Name _____

A Bear Who's Not a Bear

Everyone knows what a teddy bear looks like. A **koala** bear, who's really not a bear, looks a lot like your favorite teddy. When a koala is born he is only about an inch long. <u>He</u> crawls into his mother's pocket for six months. For three months longer he hangs on her back. This fuzzy, bushy-tailed animal eats only one kind of food. All night long he munches the leaves of the blue gum tree. During the day he sleeps in its branches. In the past the koala were hunted for their beautiful gray and white fur. Today the **Australian** government protects them.

1. **In the story, the word <u>munches</u> means:**
   a. chews
   b. sleeps
   c. mumbles

2. **Another word for <u>protects</u> is:**
   a. pumps
   b. guards
   c. affords

3. **The opposite of <u>day</u> is:**
   a. doubt
   b. able
   c. night

4. **A word in the story that sounds like <u>bare</u> is:**

   _____

5. **The word <u>he</u> stands for:**
   a. teddy bear
   b. koala bear
   c. blue gum tree

6. **A word in the story that goes with <u>weeks</u> and <u>years</u> is:**
   a. months
   b. hunted
   c. gray

★ **On the back of this paper name two other animals who live in trees. Write about why they live in trees and not on the ground.**

The American Bird

High on a cliff, bald eagle eggs are warmed by both parents. Both feed the newl[y] hatched **eaglets** and guard the nest. The eaglets' soft down turns to gray or brow[n] feathers at age two. At four, the head, neck and tail become white. The bill, feet an[d] part of the toes turn to bright yellow. In the early morning, eagles hunt for sma[ll] animals, snakes and birds. <u>They</u> eat, rest and fly. They soar faster than 100 mile[s] per hour. The bald eagle is the bird that stands for the United States. You can se[e] his picture on a dollar bill.

1. **In the story, the word <u>high</u> means:**
   a. far above the ground
   b. on the ground
   c. below the ground

2. **Another word for <u>hunt</u> is:**
   a. lose
   b. allow
   c. seek

3. **The opposite of <u>bright</u> is:**
   a. bring
   b. dull
   c. safe

4. **A word in the story that sounds like <u>sore</u> is:**

   _____

5. **The word <u>they</u> stands for:**
   a. eagles
   b. snakes
   c. dollar bills

6. **A word in the story that goes with <u>noon</u> and <u>evening</u> is:**
   a. faster
   b. picture
   c. morning

★ **The bald eagle is dying out. On the back of this paper, write what you can do to protect the eagle.**

2

FS-32045 Readi[ng]

It's Freezing Here

The **Antarctic** Ocean is a cold place to live. Yet, <u>it</u> is home to thousands of whales nd millions of seals. **Penguins** live here too. They swim with their wings to find sh for supper. Then they sun themselves on ice islands. The largest animal that ver lived in this ocean is the blue whale. This animal can grow to be longer than irteen automobiles placed end to end. Most of the water in this ocean freezes uring the winter. In October, the solid ice packs break into huge chunks.

In the story, the word <u>ocean</u> means:
a. a small body of water
b. a lake
c. a large body of water

Another word for <u>home</u> is:
a. house
b. car
c. pony

The opposite of <u>cold</u> is:
a. freezing
b. cool
c. hot

A word in the story that sounds like <u>blew</u> is:

_____

The word <u>it</u> stands for:
a. the blue whale
b. the Antarctic Ocean
c. penguins

A word in the story that goes with <u>tens</u> and <u>hundreds</u> is:
a. largest
b. thousands
c. October

Pretend you live on an ice island. On the back of this paper write about how you would live. What kind of house would you have? How about food and clothing?

Name _____

Collecting Money

Would you like to collect coins? It's an interesting hobby and you can learn many things. Coins tell the history of a country. Some show pictures of famous people, rare birds and animals. There are buildings called mints in the United States where coins are made. Each mint places a special mark on coins <u>it</u> makes. Take good care of your coins; they are worth more if they look new. Maybe you'll be lucky and find a rare one.

1. In the story, the word <u>collect</u> means:
   a. bring together
   b. take apart
   c. sharpen

2. Another word for <u>mark</u> is:
   a. make
   b. sign
   c. part

3. The opposite of <u>interesting</u> is:
   a. dull
   b. fun
   c. find

4. A word in the story that sounds like <u>maid</u> is:
   _____

5. The word <u>it</u> stands for:
   a. the mint
   b. coins
   c. birds

6. A word in the story that goes with <u>pennies</u> and <u>nickels</u> is:
   a. mark
   b. coins
   c. people

★ **On the back of this paper write about something you collect or would like to collect. Draw a picture to go with your story.**

FS-32045 Read

On a Starry Night

Long before movies or television, people looked at the stars at night. <u>They</u> gave names to groups of stars. One group of seven stars was called the Big Dipper. These stars form the shape of a cup with a long handle. The two large stars in front of the cup point to the north star. One star in the handle is a double star. When two stars circle each other they are known as a double star. Look at the night sky. Try to find the Big Dipper.

1. In the story, the word <u>handle</u> means:
   a. something on a plate
   b. something on a glass
   c. something on a cup

2. Another word for <u>find</u> is:
   a. lose
   b. discover
   c. hold

3. The opposite of <u>before</u> is:
   a. later
   b. today
   c. after

4. A word in the story that sounds like <u>inn</u> is:

   _____

5. The word <u>they</u> stands for:
   a. people who lived long ago
   b. stars
   c. Big Dipper

6. A word in the story that goes with <u>sun</u> and <u>moon</u> is:
   a. shape
   b. stars
   c. handle

★ **Imagine a group of stars. Draw a picture of them on the back of this paper. Write the name of your star group.**

Name _____

Talk to the Animals

For many years, scientists have studied how animals learn from one another. They have discovered many things. Birds, fish, monkeys, insects and other animals do talk to each other. They make signals that stand for danger and they can cry for help. They can tell others that food is waiting and where it is. Some animals do this by making sounds. Some move in a special way and some leave a scent trail. Watch some ants trail each other to a piece of candy. Rub your finger on the path. The scent trail is gone and the ants will scatter!

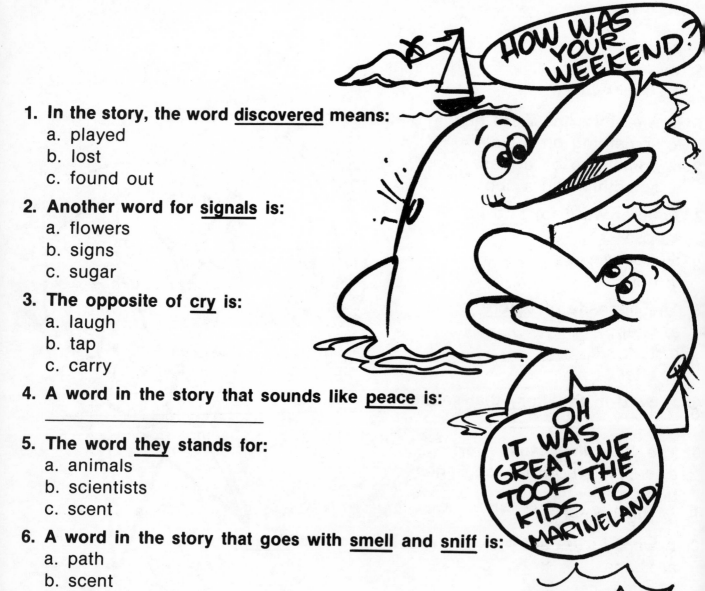

1. **In the story, the word <u>discovered</u> means:**
   a. played
   b. lost
   c. found out

2. **Another word for <u>signals</u> is:**
   a. flowers
   b. signs
   c. sugar

3. **The opposite of <u>cry</u> is:**
   a. laugh
   b. tap
   c. carry

4. **A word in the story that sounds like <u>peace</u> is:**
   _____

5. **The word <u>they</u> stands for:**
   a. animals
   b. scientists
   c. scent

6. **A word in the story that goes with <u>smell</u> and <u>sniff</u> is:**
   a. path
   b. scent
   c. piece

★ **On the back of this paper write a story about animals who really talk. Tell what they might say.**

FS-32045 Reading

Name _____

Where Does Cork Come From?

Have you ever wondered how a cork bottle stopper is made? Cork is the bark of the evergreen oak trees. These trees grow along the southern coast of **Europe.** Each time their bark is peeled, the oaks grow stronger and healthier. The cork is boiled to soften it, and then dried in sheets. Because it floats on water it is used to make life jackets. It is used to sound proof rooms because sound is trapped by cork. It can even be ground into cork flour and mixed with oil. This mixture is made into shiny floor coverings.

1. **In the story, the word <u>cork</u> means:**
   a. something that comes from flowers
   b. something that comes from animals
   c. something that comes from trees

2. **Another word for <u>trapped</u> is:**
   a. held
   b. played
   c. tossed

3. **The opposite of <u>soften</u> is:**
   a. shiny
   b. harden
   c. ribbon

4. **A word in the story that sounds like <u>maid</u> is:**

   _____

5. **The word <u>their</u> stands for:**
   a. cork
   b. jackets
   c. trees

6. **A word in the story that goes with <u>noise</u> and <u>clatter</u> is:**
   a. rooms
   b. sound
   c. shiny

★ **On the back of this paper make a list. Write everything you can think of that comes from trees. Draw some pictures to go with your list.**

The Case of the Halloween Trick

"What kind of Halloween is this?" asked Mr. Fletcher. "We give kids candy and then they steal tools from my garage." He called some of his neighbors to be on the lookout for a thief dressed as a trick-or-treater. A group of kids came to the door of the Billings house. Mrs. Billings answered the door. "What a cute costume," she told the clown, and tweaked his nose. He laughed. She yelled, "Boo!" at the ghost and he got scared. She pulled the hobo's beard and he yowled, "Ouch!" but the beard didn't come off. She jerked the devil's moustache and it fell off. "Don't leave yet, kids, the police are coming. One of you is not a child or trick-or-treater."

Who did it and how did Mrs. Billings know? _____

_____

1. **The main idea of this story is:**
   a. a devil's moustache
   b. cute costumes
   c. a phony trick-or-treater

2. **The ghost got scared because:**
   a. Someone yelled at him.
   b. He looked in a mirror.
   c. Someone stepped on his sheet.

3. **What happened to Mr. Fletcher?**

   _____

4. **The thief probably thought:**
   a. It was Christmas.
   b. He was pretty smart.
   c. Candy was awful.

5. **The devil's moustache:**
   a. got wet
   b. was sticky
   c. fell off

6. **Cute means:**
   a. charming or pretty
   b. bow-legged
   c. silly

Brainwork! On the back of this page, write a story about "The Best Halloween I Ever Had".

FS-32045 Readin

The Case of the Classroom Cheater

"Scott! Shawn! Come here immediately!" demanded Mr. Doherty. The boys went up to the teacher's desk quietly. "Both of you got eighty-nine on the science test," said Mr. Doherty, "and you both got the same answers wrong. Neither of you knew in what year the telephone was invented." Scott said, "Mr. Doherty, I didn't cheat." Shawn looked insulted. "Well, I sure didn't cheat. I knew everything about Tom Edison and his telephone." Mr. Doherty shook his head. "I know who cheated," he said.

Who did it and how did Mr. Doherty know? _____

_____

_____

1. **The main idea of this story is:**
   a. flunking a test
   b. a boy who cheated
   c. a great invention

2. **Both boys:**
   a. got all the questions right
   b. got the same score
   c. were brothers

3. **Why did the teacher want to see the boys?**

   _____

4. **You can tell that:**
   a. Both boys lied.
   b. Kids always cheat.
   c. One of the boys lied.

5. **What kind of test did the boys take?**

   a. science   b. math   c. swimming

6. **Immediately means:**
   a. tomorrow
   b. yesterday
   c. right away

Brainwork! Think about the question and answer it on the back.
What should Mr. Doherty do next?

The Mystery of Mother's Note

Henry was in trouble again. His teacher, Ms. Haggerty, had given him a note to take home to his mother. The note said, "Dear Mrs. Simpson, Henry is failing all his subjects, especially spelling and math. He is not trying at all. Sincerely, Ms. Haggerty." Oh, boy, thought Henry. Am I going to get it! Hey! I'll write a different note. "Dear Mrs. Simpson, Henry is doing well in awl his subjects, expecialy speling and math." Henry gave the note to his mom. "Henry!" she yelled. "Wait until your father gets home. You wrote this note, not your teacher!"

How did Mrs. Simpson know that her son had written the note? _____

1. **The main idea of this story is:**
   a. a good math student
   b. a boy in trouble
   c. a note for Father

2. **How was Henry doing in school?**
   a. very well
   b. pretty well
   c. very poorly

3. **Which words in the note did Henry misspell?** _____

   _____

4. **You can tell that Henry thinks he is:**

   a. pretty smart   b. very tall   c. a teacher

5. **Henry decided to write:**
   a. a Christmas card
   b. a different note
   c. a letter to his teacher

6. <u>**Sincerely**</u> **means:**
   a. happily
   b. sadly
   c. honestly

Brainwork! Think about the question and answer it on the back.
What should Henry tell his father when he gets home?

The Case of the Missing Milk

Now for a glass of cold chocolate milk, thought Jason. He poured himself a full glass and had one gulp. Just then the phone rang. When Jason came back, the glass was empty! Maybe, he thought, his brother Toby drank it. Suddenly, Jason's cat, Muffin, ran across the room. She started to clean her whiskers, which looked brown. "Aha," Jason said out loud. "Muffin stuck her whole nose and mouth in my glass and drank all the milk! Muffin, why didn't you tell me you wanted some?" he laughed.

How did Jason know that Muffin had drunk his milk? _____

_____

1. The main idea of this story is:
   a. a cat that liked milk
   b. a glass of water
   c. a phone call

2. Jason left his milk because:
   a. Muffin wanted her dinner.
   b. His mother wanted him.
   c. He heard the telephone.

3. At first, what did Jason think?

   _____

4. You can tell that:
   a. Jason shouted at Muffin.
   b. Jason wasn't angry.
   c. Jason's friend called.

5. How did Muffin's whiskers look?
   a. brown   b. stiff   c. gray

6. Whiskers are:
   a. milk on your face
   b. dirt on your face
   c. hair on your face

Brainwork! Think about the question and answer it on the back.
How could you write this story with a different ending?

11   FS-32045 Reading

The Case of the Missing Pearls

Nellie loved her new pearls. She wore them every day. At night she hid them in her sewing box. She thought that would be the last place that burglars would look. Aunt Jenny came to visit. She said she'd be glad to do some mending for Nellie. The next morning Nellie went to get her pearls. They were gone! Could the milkman or the plumber have taken them? Aunt Jenny came into the room. "Here's your dress that I mended, Nellie. It was missing some buttons, so I used those large white ones in your sewing box." Nellie screamed, "Oh, no!"

Who did it and how did Nellie know? _____

_____

1. **The main idea of this story is:**
   a. a milkman
   b. a new dress
   c. a good place for pearls

2. **Nellie didn't want burglars to:**
   a. take her pearls
   b. stay for tea
   c. leave her house

3. **What did Aunt Jenny want to do?**

_____

4. **You can tell that Aunt Jenny:**
   a. is a plumber
   b. doesn't like to sew
   c. doesn't see too well

5. **Nellie hid her pearls:**
   a. all day
   b. at night
   c. in the attic

6. **Pearls are:**
   a. a kind of bird
   b. white gems made by oysters
   c. pieces of gold and silver

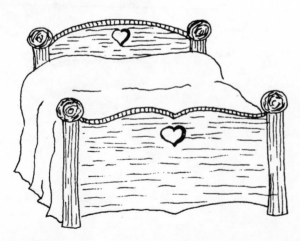

Brainwork! Think about the question and answer it on the back.
What would be a better place to hide Nellie's pearls?

12

The Case of the Missing Book

"Janice, will you read your book report first?" asked Mrs. Damon. Janice lushed. "I couldn't do it, Mrs. Damon. The book I chose, "A Horse of a ifferent Color," disappeared. I had it on my desk but someone took it." The ids took out their reports. Marvin's was about a lost dog. Miriam's was bout a purple horse. Sally's was about a shipwrecked family named obinson. Dana's was called "The Great Brain." Janice almost couldn't wait ntil the reports ended. She raised her hand. "Mrs. Damon, I know who took y book. Miriam did." Miriam said she was sorry. "I wanted to get that book, ut you got it first," she said.

How did Janice know that Miriam had taken her book? _____

_____

The main idea of this story is:
a. a purple cat
b. book reports
c. a lost dog

2. Janice didn't do her report because:
a. Her book was gone.
b. The teacher wouldn't let her.
c. She didn't know how to read.

3. Janice's book was called:

_____

4. Janice's book was probably:
a. a true story
b. a silly story
c. a story about people

5. Who reported on "The Great Brain"?
a. Janice
b. Mrs. Damon
c. Dana

6. Blushed means:
a. turned white
b. turned blue
c. turned red

Brainwork! On the back of this page, write a story called "A Horse of a Different Color".

The Case of the Broken Window

Mr. Phillips sat in his living room, reading his paper. Suddenly, there was a loud crash! A baseball came sailing through the window. Mr. Phillips took the ball and went outside. Some boys were playing in the street. "OK, who did it?" Mr. Phillips asked. "I didn't see it happen," said Bob. "Neither did I," said Sam. "I heard a noise," added Paul. "I wasn't near your living room," said Bill. "I don't play baseball," declared John. "I know who did it now," Mr. Phillips said.

Who did it and how did Mr. Phillips know? _____

1. **The main idea of this story is:**
   a. some noisy kids
   b. a baseball game
   c. the truth about a window

2. **Sam claimed that:**
   a. He didn't see the crime happen.
   b. He threw the baseball.
   c. He didn't know Mr. Phillips.

3. **What was Mr. Phillips doing?**
   _____

4. **You can tell that Mr. Phillips:**
   a. was very happy
   b. felt angry
   c. threw the baseball himself

5. **Paul admitted he'd:**
   a. seen the whole thing
   b. gone to sleep
   c. heard a noise

6. **Frowning means:**
   a. smiling and cheering
   b. wrinkling your brow
   c. screaming out loud

Brainwork! Think about the question and answer it on the back.
What do you think Mr. Phillips should do about the person who broke his window?

FS-32045 Readi

P.T. or Not P.T.?

The Andersons woke up late one Sunday morning. Cindy Anderson went outside. "Oh, no!" she yelled. Her parents came running. They gasped. Someone had covered their tree with rolls and rolls of paper towels! It had rained and now they were all stuck to the tree. Cindy called her friends. They were going shopping for their club picnic later. Alice would buy ketchup. Harriette listed fruit and milk. Sandra's list said hot dogs and six rolls of paper towels which her mother had asked her to get. Nora would buy the hot dog buns. "I know who messed up our tree," said Cindy.

Who did it and how did Cindy know? _____

_____

1. **The main idea of this story is:**
   a. a long list
   b. a funny tree
   c. a mean trick

2. **During the night the towels got:**
   a. wet
   b. blown away
   c. dry

3. **What had happened to the tree?**

   _____

4. **Cindy will probably:**
   a. laugh at the whole thing
   b. not want to be Sandra's friend
   c. tell her friends to go home

5. **Who would buy the hot dog buns?**
   a. Sandra
   b. Nora
   c. Cindy

6. **Gasped means:**
   a. to cry
   b. draw in the breath sharply
   c. to hold your breath for a long time

Brainwork! Think about the question and answer it on the back.
If a friend of yours "P.T.'d" your tree, what would you do?

15   FS-32045 Reading

The Case of the Missing Flowers

"Allen Bloom!" yelled Mrs. Di Bento, Allen's neighbor. "I know you took my flowers. I never give them to anyone. You picked them!" Allen said he didn't, but Mrs. Di Bento wouldn't believe him. Just then, Mrs. Di Bento's son, Darrell, came home from school. A note was in his hand. It fell to the ground. Allen picked it up. It said, Dear Mrs. Di Bento, Thank you for the flowers. Signed, Mrs. Lovelady, Darrell's teacher. "Darrell took your flowers," said Allen. "I'm sorry I accused you," blushed Mrs. Di Bento.

How did Allen know that Darrell took the flowers? _____

_____

1. **The main idea of this story is:**
   a. daisies and pansies
   b. falsely accused
   c. a blushing neighbor

2. **Darrell was carrying:**
   a. a bunch of flowers
   b. a thank-you note
   c. his report card

3. **Of what did Mrs. Di Bento accuse Allen?**

   _____

4. **You can tell that Darrell:**
   a. wanted to make his mother mad
   b. wanted to get Allen in trouble
   c. wanted to please his teacher

5. **Mrs. Di Bento was:**
   a. Darrell's neighbor
   b. Allen's sister
   c. Allen's neighbor

6. **Accuse means:**
   a. saying someone did something
   b. yelling at someone
   c. calling the police

Brainwork! Think about the question and answer it on the back. What would you say to Mrs. Di Bento if you were Allen?

FS-32045 Readin

Curlock Soams and the Pilfered Pie

Curlock Soams and Dr. Spotson were eating at Pierre's Place, a famous restaurant. "And now, Mr. Soams," beamed Pierre, "my specialty, pickled prune pie." Pierre lifted the lid on the pie plate. "It is gone!" he shrieked, fainting with a thud on the floor. "None of you chaps leave the room," ordered Curlock. "Who else had this dessert tonight?" Pierre sighed, sitting up. "I prepared it just for you." Soams looked around. The customers at table two had yellow stains on their ties. Another customer was wiping whipped cream off her face. The man at table five put his black-stained handkerchief back into his pocket. "Aha," said Soams. "I've done it again."

Who did it and how did Soams know? _____

_____

1. The main idea of this story is:
   a. a man who fainted
   b. a missing pie
   c. whipped cream and pie

2. What was in the pie plate?
   a. cream pie
   b. pumpkin pie
   c. nothing

3. When Pierre saw the empty pie plate he

_____

4. You can tell that Curlock is:
   a. very fond of pie
   b. a good detective
   c. a great cook

5. What was Pierre's specialty?
   a. pickled prune pie
   b. pecan pie
   c. pelican pie

6. Pilfered means:
   a. eaten   b. stolen   c. broken

Brainwork! On the back of this page, make up a silly kind of pie and list what would be in it.

FS-32045 Reading

The Case of the Missing Sandwich

Sara brought her favorite lunch to school today. It is a peanut butter and banana sandwich. She wouldn't tell any of her friends what she had. They would all want a bite. At lunch, Sara excitedly opened her lunch box. Hey! Tuna! Someone had switched sandwiches! Sara said, "Someone took my sandwich and I don't like tuna!" Her friends said they were sorry. Kevin said, "Who would want peanut butter and banana, anyway?" Sara jumped up. "You took it, Kevin!" Kevin told Sara he would bring her a new sandwich tomorrow.

How did Sara know that Kevin had taken her sandwich? _____

_____

1. **The main idea of this story is:**
   a. a tuna sandwich
   b. late for lunch
   c. switching sandwiches

2. **With whom did Sara eat lunch?**
   a. her teacher
   b. her brother
   c. some friends

3. **What kind of sandwich did Sara like?**

   _____

4. **Kevin probably:**
   a. wanted to be mean
   b. wanted to try the sandwich
   c. didn't like sandwiches

5. **Sara thought her friends:**
   a. would want a bite
   b. would want to play
   c. like to take things

6. **Switched means:**
   a. to keep
   b. to exchange
   c. to eat

Brainwork! Think about the question and answer it on the back.
Why do you think Kevin didn't just ask Sara to share her sandwich?

18   FS-32045 Reading

The Case of the Missing Dog

The phone rang loudly. Curlock Soams grouchily rose from his comfy chair. "Hello! Mr. Soams!" came a panicky voice over the phone. "My valuable dog has been stolen!" It was Curlock's neighbor, Mrs. Broomhead. The detective sprang into action. No one in the neighborhood but Mrs. Broomhead had a dog. Curlock walked around the block. Mrs. Singer had cans of cat food falling out of her garbage cans. Poor Mr. Dingman had a mess in his driveway. Dog food was falling out of a big sack. The Robinsons had sacks of birdseed near their side door. "By Jove!" shouted Curlock. "I've cracked the case."

Who did it and how did Curlock know? _____

---

1. **The main idea of this story is:**
   a. a grouchy detective
   b. finding a dognapper
   c. eating birdseed

2. **What was Curlock doing?**
   a. feeding his cat
   b. playing his violin
   c. sitting in a chair

3. **Who had a mess in his driveway?**

   _____

4. **You can tell that the dognapper:**
   a. lived in the neighborhood
   b. was a bird
   c. had a pet shop

5. **Curlock decided to:**
   a. take a dog
   b. take a walk
   c. take a nap

6. **Panicky means:**
   a. terrified
   b. itchy
   c. funny

Brainwork! Think about the question and answer it on the back.
Why would someone take a dog?

19

The Case of the Vicious Vandals

Some awful people had broken into the school. There was damage to some classrooms and things were missing. Two typewriters had been taken from the office. Mrs. Loomis, the school secretary, said one of the typewriters had a broken key. "The C key is broken and all the C's look like G's." Mr. Chester's English class was getting ready to turn in their stories. "Pass them all in, please," asked the teacher. He looked them over. "I noticed that some people typed their stories. Susan, yours, "The Cat and the Dog," is very neat. Gary, "The Gat and the Garrot" is unusual. Harold, "The Broken Umbrella" looks great. By the way, I know who one of the vandals is."

Who did it and how did the teacher know? _____

_____

_____

1. **The main idea of this story is:**
   a. finding the vandal
   b. a broken umbrella
   c. an English class

2. **Mr. Chester asked his class to:**
   a. type their papers
   b. go to recess
   c. turn in their papers

3. **Two typewriters were**

   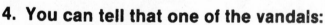

4. **You can tell that one of the vandals:**
   a. was a fifth grader
   b. was in English class
   c. was laughing

5. **The school was broken into:**
   a. on Friday
   b. by girls
   c. by awful people

6. **<u>Vandals</u> are people who:**
   a. rob banks
   b. destroy property
   c. clean schools

Brainwork! Think about the question and answer it on the back.
What do you think should be done about vandals?

20

The Case of the Missing Piece

"Ready for the Monopoly game?" asked Anita. "OK," said Alfie. They took out the set. "My favorite piece is this tiny blue truck," said Alfie. "Mine is the little pair of scissors," said Anita, "but it seems to be gone. Who took it?" Anita's other brother, Algie, was crying in the next room. "Mom, will you please tell him to be quiet?" asked Anita. "He's only two, Anita," said her mother, "and I told him he's too small to cut paper. Now he insists he has something special and won't hurt himself." Anita smiled. "I think I solved my mystery," she said.

Who did it and how did Anita know? _____

_____

1. The main idea of this story is:
   a. a small blue truck
   b. a noisy brother
   c. a missing pair of scissors

2. The pair of scissors was:
   a. big
   b. not in the game box
   c. left outside

3. Anita's brothers were named

_____

4. You can tell that:
   a. Algie is older than Anita.
   b. Anita's mother likes Monopoly.
   c. Algie is the youngest.

5. Anita wanted her brother to be:
   a. gone
   b. quiet
   c. tall

6. A favorite is:
   a. the one you like best
   b. the one you don't like
   c. the one you break

Brainwork! Think about the question and answer it on the back.
What will happen when Algie tries to cut with his "special scissors"?

The Case of the Missing Pencil

"Oh, no!" shouted Pamela. "Someone took my red pencil. I'm the only one in the class who has one. All of you have green pencils." No one admitted taking the pencil. Pamela borrowed a pencil from Grace. "Adam, please bring me a piece of green drawing paper," asked Mrs. Fisk. When Adam brought the paper, the teacher smiled. "I forgot that you're color blind, Adam. That paper is red." Suddenly, Pamela jumped up. "Adam took my pencil, but I'm sure it was a mistake. Sure, here it is on his desk." Adam looked puzzled.

How did Pamela know Adam had taken her pencil? _____

_____

_____

1. The main idea of this story is:
   a. a big pencil
   b. taken by mistake
   c. a nice teacher

2. Adam brought Mrs. Fisk
   a. the wrong color paper
   b. a blue pencil
   c. his math paper

3. Pamela borrowed a pencil from

_____

4. You can tell that Adam:
   a. always took pencils
   b. yelled at Pamela
   c. didn't know he had the red pencil

5. Mrs. Fisk had forgotten:
   a. her car keys
   b. that Adam wasn't smart
   c. that Adam was color blind

6. <u>Denied</u> means:
   a. said something wasn't true
   b. hurt his knee
   c. stole something

Brainwork! Think about the question and answer it on the back.
How could Adam keep from mistaking red pencils for green ones?

FS-32045 Readi

The Case of the Missing Lunch Money

Mrs. Kimball had told her class never to leave money in their desks. Carl's mother ad given him a ten-dollar bill and told him to bring her the change. Carl put the noney in his desk. At lunchtime, he reached into the desk. He came up with a piece f paper that said, "Thanks for the money." Carl stood up and yelled, "My money is jone! My mother will be angry." Mrs. Kimball asked, "Did anyone see Carl's money? won't say how much is missing." Annie said, "I found a dime today." Jane added, Maybe he lost his money." Arnold said, "He shouldn't have brought ten dollars to chool." Pete said, "Ten dollars? Wow!" Mrs. Kimball frowned. "I know who took the noney."

Who did it and how did the teacher know? _____

_____

. **The main idea of this story is:**
a. finding a quarter
b. a careless boy
c. an angry mother

. **Carl knew his mother would be:**
a. happy
b. funny
c. angry

. **What had Carl taken to school?**

_____

. **You can tell that Carl was:**
a. careful b. laughing c. careless

. **Carl left his money in his:**
a. shoe
b. desk
c. wallet

. **Frowned means:**
a. smile
b. bring your brows together
c. sniff in the air

Brainwork! Think about the question and answer it on the back.
What should Carl have done to make sure no one took his money?

Name _____ Date _____

The Case of the Ghostly Visit

Jack and Beatrice had bet their friends that they would go to the old Bramble house. Everyone knew the place was haunted. Jack and Beatrice entered the house. The door creaked and there were spiderwebs all over the place. Suddenly, a white figure jumped out and yelled, "Boo! Leave my house, you two!" The kids ran screaming all the way home. The next day was windy. All the neighbors' clothing was hanging on lines, drying in the breeze. Jimmy Jones' lines had lots of diapers on them. Sam Silver's had lots of sheets. One of them needed patching because it had two large holes in it. Susan Small's line had tiny doll clothes on it. Beatrice and Jack looked at each other. They knew the ghost's secret.

Who did it and how did the kids know? _____

_____

1. The main idea of this story is:
   a. finding a ghost
   b. a stiff wind
   c. creaking doors and spiderwebs

2. The ghost told the kids to:
   a. make him a sandwich
   b. close the door
   c. get out of the house

3. Where were Jack and Beatrice going?

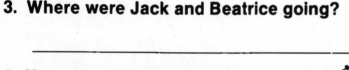

4. You can tell that the kids:
   a. weren't scared at all
   b. really were scared
   c. loved ghosts

5. What was hanging on lines?
   a. telephones
   b. clothes
   c. pictures

6. Figure means:
   a. ghost b. shape c. house

Brainwork! On the back of this page, write a ghost story in two paragraphs.

24   FS-32045 Readi

The Case of the Ruined Birthday

World-famous detective Curlock Soams was getting ready for his niece ridget's surprise birthday party. Suddenly, there was a knock at the door. Curlock!" yelled his sister. "The cake I made is missing! All six layers of it! he birthday is ruined!" "Not to worry, my dear. Spotson and I will solve this ase." Curlock was soon joined by his able assistant, Dr. Spotson. "I do have n idea, Spotson," said Curlock. "Let's go to Barker's Bakery." Spotson was uzzled. "But Curlock, they have awful cakes." "Oh, Mr. Soams," said Barker. hear your niece is having a birthday. I just happen to have a birthday cake ll ready." "Just a minute, Barker," frowned Curlock. "You stole my niece's ake and now you want to sell it back to me."

How did Curlock know Mr. Barker did it? _____

The main idea of this story is:
a. a bad baker
b. a missing cake
c. a great party

Soams knew he could:
a. find the answer
b. sing "Happy Birthday"
c. eat some cake

Who joined Curlock?

5. Barker's cakes were:
a. delicious
b. awful
c. gone

6. An <u>assistant</u> is:
a. a cake
b. a boss
c. a helper

You can tell that:
a. Curlock likes chocolate.
b. Bridget is ten years old.
c. Curlock is very helpful.

Brainwork! Think about the question and answer it on the back. What did Curlock do after he found the cake thief?

The Case of the April Fool's Joke

"Look out, everyone," warned Mr. Jenkins. "Today is April Fool's Day. I hope that no one will play jokes that are mean." Later that day, the joke was on Mr. Jenkins. As he sat down, he slid right onto the floor. "Someone put oil on that chair. Now my pants have an oil stain, and that's very hard to get out." Later, Mr. Jenkins called on some students to do math problems. Alma had eaten a jelly sandwich for lunch. She left some jelly on the board. "Will the board monitor please wipe off the board?" asked the teacher. Tommy did his job but his hand left a big, greasy mark on the board. "Now, that's worse," said Mr. Jenkins, "but I have solved the mystery of the April Fool's joke."

Whodunit and how did Mr. Jenkins know? _____

_____

1. The main idea of this story is:
   a. a board with jelly
   b. a mean joke
   c. a teacher that got hurt

2. What happened to Mr. Jenkins?
   a. He fell out of his chair.
   b. He got jelly on his chin.
   c. He fell and cried.

3. What did Tommy leave on the board?

   _____

4. Mr. Jenkins probably felt:
   a. happy   b. angry   c. mean

5. What did Alma leave on the board?
   a. the chalk
   b. a math problem
   c. some jelly

6. A <u>stain</u> is:
   a. a kind of meat
   b. a spot
   c. a country in Europe

Brainwork! Think about the question and answer it on the back.
Make a list of April Fool's jokes you'd like to play.

The Greatest

Muhammad Ali was the first heavyweight boxing **champion** to win the **title** three times. He was one of the most interesting stars in sports. Muhammad called himself "The Greatest".

Muhammad Ali became famous after he won a Gold Medal in the Olympic Games of 1960. Besides boxing, Ali has written a book about himself. He also wrote funny **poems** which teased the people he boxed. Sometimes he acted on TV and in movies.

Spending his time helping children is important to Ali. He tells them that if they try hard they can do well in life, too. In 1978 Muhammad lost his title. Later that year he got it back. In 1979 Muhammad Ali retired from boxing, still the champ.

1. **The main idea of this story is:**
   a. Muhammad Ali was a real champion.
   b. Boxing is fun.
   c. Muhammad Ali writes poems.

2. **Muhammad says:**
   a. He can play baseball.
   b. He is great.
   c. People tease him.

3. **When did Muhammad Ali become famous?**
   a. when he was a baby
   b. when he wrote a book
   c. after the Olympic Games

4. **What word means <u>to make fun of, to laugh at someone</u>?**
   a. title
   b. tease
   c. box

5. **The story doesn't say, but Muhammad Ali probably:**
   a. trained very hard to become a good boxer
   b. likes ice cream and cake
   c. is very skinny

Stars from the Good Old Days

The picture on TV looks kind of fuzzy. Don't try to fix it! This show wa[s] made in the 1930's. The film is very old. The "Little **Rascals**" you see on T[V] used to be called "The Our Gang **Comedies**".

The Rascals were a group of kids. They did funny things and got int[o] trouble. They had funny names, too. **Alfalfa** was tall and skinny. He tried to b[e] very serious. Spanky was chubby with a funny voice. Darla was the only gi[rl] member of the gang. Even today, these kids and their mischief are fun t[o] watch.

Stan **Laurel** and **Oliver** Hardy also made movies in the 1930's and 1940'[s]. Oliver, tall and fat, always picked on Laurel, the skinny one. Sometimes Laurel made Hardy look silly. They did things like trip each other and fa[ll] down. Sometimes they'd get pies thrown in their faces. More than forty year[s] later, they still make us laugh.

1. The main idea of this story is:
   a. Hardy was fat.
   b. TV pictures sometimes look fuzzy.
   c. Old-time stars still make us laugh.

2. The "Little Rascals" were:
   a. children
   b. bears
   c. girls

3. The "Little Rascals" always got into:
   a. candy
   b. school
   c. trouble

4. Another word for <u>skinny</u> is:
   a. green
   b. thin
   c. chubby

5. We probably laugh at "pies-in-the-face" because:
   a. They look tasty.
   b. You shouldn't waste food.
   c. People look silly with pie on their faces.

Comic Book Heroes

You know Superman, Batman, Wonder Woman and Spiderman. They've all been on TV. Superman even had a movie made about his life. Don't forget "The **Incredible** Hulk", either.

All these "super heroes" are fun to see. Superman can fly. Batman and Robin have so many tricks. Wonder Woman has magic **bracelets** and a rope. They protect her and help catch bad guys, too. Spiderman is amazing. He can climb up buildings. And the Hulk is so strong!

These famous heroes started out in comic books. People liked their adventures very much. Television shows were made about them. Sometimes they seem very real. We even know the story of Superman's whole life. It would be fun to see him really speeding through the sky!

1. **The main idea of this story is:**
   a. about super heroes
   b. about comic books
   c. climbing up buildings

2. **Wonder Woman's bracelets:**
   a. help keep her safe
   b. are gold
   c. look nice

3. **The super heroes started out in:**
   a. movies
   b. radio
   c. comic books

4. **A hulk is:**
   a. a green plant
   b. a forest animal
   c. a big, clumsy person

5. **Super heroes probably:**
   a. always win
   b. never win
   c. are crybabies

A Man Who Cared

Roberto Clemente was born in Puerto Rico. When he was young he came to the United States. When he grew up he became one of the best baseball players ever.

Roberto won four batting **titles**. He played on twelve all-star teams. In 197 he was named the best player in the World Series. He was the eleventh man in history to get 3,000 hits.

Roberto played baseball for eighteen happy years. But he cared about people, too. In 1972 a strong **earthquake** hit the country of **Nicaragua**. Many people were killed or left homeless. Roberto wanted to help. He flew to Nicaragua. On the way there, his plane crashed and he was killed. Roberto Clemente was a great ball player and a great person.

1. **The main idea of this story is:**
   a. Roberto Clemente was a great person.
   b. Many people got 3,000 hits.
   c. Baseball players are nice.

2. **Roberto Clemente:**
   a. wanted to be a farmer
   b. liked helping people
   c. played soccer

3. **Roberto was born in:**
   a. New York
   b. California
   c. Puerto Rico

4. **An earthquake is:**
   a. movement of the earth
   b. a big storm
   c. the sound a duck makes

5. **You can tell that Roberto Clemente:**
   a. wanted to stop playing baseball
   b. liked playing baseball
   c. was six feet tall

FS-32045 Reading

A Musical Wonder

He sings rock and other **music**. He writes his own songs and plays many instruments. Stevie Wonder does these things very well. Yet he has been blind all his life.

Stevie has been able to overcome his blindness. He wrote and recorded his first song at age twelve. At that time Stevie's songs were very lively. Stevie also writes serious songs.

Stevie's songs sell millions of records. He has many gold records. Gold records are given to people whose record sales are more than one million. Stevie has also won more than fifteen **Grammy Awards**. This award is given for writing, singing or playing music. Stevie Wonder has become famous all over the world.

1. **The main idea of this story is:**
   a. People buy records.
   b. Children write songs.
   c. Stevie Wonder is a famous singing star.

2. **Gold records are given:**
   a. to dairy farmers
   b. for songs that sell lots of records
   c. to movie stars

3. **Stevie writes his own:**
   a. books
   b. letters
   c. songs

4. **Music means:**
   a. a pleasing combination of sounds
   b. a kind of paper
   c. a person

5. **From this story you can tell that:**
   a. Stevie loves music.
   b. Stevie is six feet tall.
   c. Stevie was born in Michigan.

Kermit, Miss Piggy and Friends

Kermit the Frog and Miss Piggy seem like real people. So do the rest of tha **gang** called "The **Muppets**". Jim Henson started the Muppets in the 1950's. I was a new idea in puppets. Some Muppets are small and some are as large as real people. The Muppets stand on a stage and are moved from below. Each Muppet is worked by a different person.

Kermit and Miss Piggy are the most famous Muppets. Miss Piggy thinks she's beautiful. She wants people to **admire** her. Kermit was the first Muppe Jim Henson was the voice of Kermit. Miss Piggy always runs after Kermit.

The muppets became so famous they had a TV show and made movies.

1. The main idea of this story is:
   a. Miss Piggy is pretty.
   b. Kermit is green.
   c. The Muppets are big stars.

2. The Muppets are worked by:
   a. two people who hop around a lot
   b. many different people
   c. elves who live under the stage

3. The man who started the Muppets was:
   a. Jim Henson
   b. Kermit the Frog
   c. George Washington

4. Famous means:
   a. liking cookies
   b. being known by many people
   c. blowing up balloons

5. The Muppets are probably well-liked because:
   a. They're all different colors.
   b. People like pigs.
   c. They are funny.

Marathon Man

Children run every day at home and at school. But what is it like to run in a **marathon** race? It's 26 miles of running without stopping. Thousands of men and women run to beat you, too. In the 1960's people began jogging. By the 1970's everyone got faster! Running became a big sport. Now cities all over America have races. Some are short, only ten **kilometers**. Others, like those in Boston and New York, are marathons.

Bill Rodgers has been in many marathons. In 1979 he won his fourth New York Marathon. More than 11,000 people ran against him! Bill ran the 26 miles in 2 hours, 11 minutes and 42 seconds.

Bill Rodgers has also won the Boston Marathon and many others. Running is a good sport. All you need are good running shoes and comfortable clothes.

1. **The main idea of this story is:**
   a. good running shoes
   b. about Boston and New York
   c. about running and Bill Rodgers

2. **Marathon running is done by:**
   a. many people
   b. women only
   c. a few people

3. **By 1979 how many New York Marathons had Bill Rodgers won?**
   a. 10
   b. 2
   c. 4

4. **A kilometer is:**
   a. a kind of measurement
   b. a kind of shoe
   c. a kind of sport

5. **In order to win a marathon race, you should:**
   a. practice running long distances
   b. buy some running shorts
   c. watch lots of TV

One Giant Step for Mankind

Imagine being the first person to set foot on the moon! Neil **Armstrong** wa the lucky one! In 1969, **astronauts** Armstrong and Edwin E. Aldrin, Jr., lande on the moon. They gathered dirt and rocks. **Millions** of people saw it on TV

Going to the moon wasn't Neil's first time in space. In 1969 he and Davi Scott had docked two ships in space for the first time. While they wer aboard, one ship began to shake. But they knew what they were doing. The stopped the shaking and landed safely.

The first moon landing was very important. We found out what the moo was made of. The flight proved that we could visit other planets. Neil Armstrong was a real space **pioneer**.

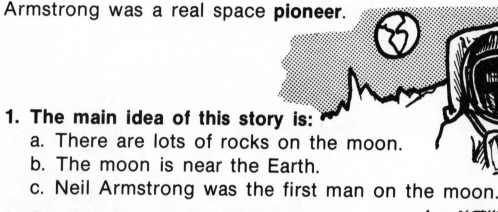

1. **The main idea of this story is:**
   a. There are lots of rocks on the moon.
   b. The moon is near the Earth.
   c. Neil Armstrong was the first man on the moon.

2. **Sending men to the moon was:**
   a. important
   b. silly
   c. boring

3. **What was found on the moon?**
   a. green cheese
   b. cars
   c. dirt and rocks

4. **An astronaut is:**
   a. a rock star
   b. a traveler in space
   c. a candy bar

5. **Since we found out that we can travel in space, we'll probably:**
   a. stay home from now on
   b. try to reach far-off planets someday soon
   c. sell moon rocks

"Heyyy, It's the Fonz!"

The Fonz comes into the soda shop. He snaps his fingers and music comes from the **jukebox**. Everyone likes the Fonz. He's always around when needed.

The real name of the Fonz is Arthur **Fonzarelli**, but his friends call him "the Fonz" or "Fonzie". He fixes cars better than anyone. His best friends, the **Cunninghams**, treat him like one of the family. Fonzie pretends to be tough, but he is really kind and gentle.

The actor who played Fonzie on the show "Happy Days" is Henry **Winkler**. Henry also plays many other roles in movies and TV. He does other things, too. Henry tells people about special children. Many of these children can't walk, see or hear. But they like to play and have fun, too. Henry Winkler cares about people. He is just as nice as the Fonz.

1. **The main idea of this story is:**
   a. about Henry Winkler
   b. TV shows
   c. things children can do

2. **The Fonz likes to:**
   a. help people
   b. eat candy
   c. sing songs

3. **Who does Henry Winkler tell people about?**
   a. whales
   b. special children
   c. truck drivers

4. **A jukebox is:**
   a. a package
   b. a kind of snake
   c. a big record player

5. **The story doesn't tell:**
   a. what Fonzie wears
   b. Fonzie's real name
   c. the name of Fonzie's friends

An American Hero

John **Wayne** made more than 175 movies in his life. The first time he was in a movie was in 1928. But John didn't become famous until 1939. After that, whenever someone needed a cowboy star, he was called. He also made many war and police movies.

People all over the world thought of John Wayne as a hero. He **reminded** them of all the good things about Americans. Some Americans became angry with John Wayne, though. He felt that Americans should fight the war in **Vietnam**. Many people didn't agree. But they knew he was brave to speak his mind.

John Wayne won an "Oscar" for being the best actor of 1969. In 1979, just before he died, he was given a medal. The United States gives this medal to people who serve their country well.

1. **The main idea of this story is:**
   a. Cowboys like horses.
   b. Oscars are given to good actors.
   c. John Wayne was liked by many people.

2. **People felt that John Wayne:**
   a. was a good American
   b. shouldn't have made movies
   c. was a good swimmer

3. **John Wayne starred in:**
   a. cowboy movies
   b. musical movies
   c. movies about animals

4. **Reminded means:**
   a. to babysit
   b. to make someone remember
   c. to listen carefully

5. **From the story you can tell that:**
   a. Movie stars like to be cowboys.
   b. John Wayne was proud to be an American.
   c. Movies are hard to make.

Everybody Loves Lucy

It's time for "I Love Lucy". Every day millions of people watch **Lucille** Ball on television. But this show was first shown on TV in 1951!

Children still love Lucy although these old shows aren't even in color. Lucy is funny. Strange and **amusing** things always happen to her. She's always getting herself in trouble.

Lucille Ball began acting in the movies in the 1930's. She was in plays, too. At first she didn't do funny parts. Then people found out she could make them laugh. Lucy and her husband were given their own TV show. People like to watch Lucy, her family and their neighbors. Fifty years from now "I Love Lucy" will probably still be on TV!

1. **The main idea of this story is:**
   a. "Lucy" isn't in color.
   b. TV shows are funny.
   c. "Lucy" is a show people like.

2. **Lucille Ball was good at:**
   a. playing baseball
   b. doing funny things on TV
   c. knitting

3. **What always happens on "I Love Lucy"?**
   a. Lucy gets into trouble.
   b. Lucy goes to school.
   c. Lucy goes to the store.

4. **Amusing means:**
   a. feeling sad
   b. something funny
   c. being mean

5. **You can guess that:**
   a. "Lucy" is on late at night.
   b. "Lucy" is a police show.
   c. Lucille Ball liked to make people laugh.

Name _____ Date _____

Soccer Champ

Pelé was known as the world's best soccer player. He was born to a poor family in **Brazil**. Like most people in his country, he loves soccer. He was such a good player that he became rich and famous. Pelé proved that a person from a poor family can **succeed**. Everyone in Brazil is very proud of him.

Pelé played on three world **championship** teams. He **retired** in 1974. Then he came to America. In 1977 Pelé led his new team, the New York Cosmos, to a championship. After that he retired for good.

Pelé is still famous, though. The whole world knows who he is. It will be a long time before anyone takes Pelé's place in soccer.

1. The main idea of this story is:
 a. Soccer is a good sport.
 b. Pelé was a great soccer player.
 c. Playing soccer makes you rich.

2. Soccer in Brazil:
 a. is played by poor people only
 b. is played by many bad players
 c. is very well-liked

3. Why did Pelé come to America?
 a. to see New York
 b. to play soccer
 c. to sing

4. To retire in this story means:
 a. to work hard
 b. to put new tires on your car
 c. to stop working

5. How do soccer fans probably feel about Pelé?
 a. They think he's the greatest.
 b. They don't know who he is.
 c. They don't like him.

FS-32045 Reading

The First Home Run King

The first great home run hitter in baseball was George **Herman** Ruth. veryone called him "Babe". Babe started out as a pitcher. Soon it was scovered that he was even better as a hitter. Before Babe's time, players did ot hit home runs very often. Babe made baseball more exciting by hitting homers". Soon other players began trying to hit the ball as far as Babe did.

Babe Ruth joined the New York **Yankees** in 1920. Many people came to the ames just to see him play. Soon Yankee **Stadium** was called "The House at Ruth Built".

In his life Babe hit 714 home runs. It was 40 years before this home run cord was broken! Babe retired in 1935. The next year he was chosen for the ational Baseball Hall of Fame.

The main idea of this story is:
a. "Babe" is a strange name.
b. Baseball is played in Yankee Stadium.
c. Babe Ruth was a great baseball player.

Babe Ruth:
a. made people want to watch the Yankees
b. liked cars
c. was a great skater

Babe was chosen for:
a. bubble gum cards
b. the Hall of Fame
c. movie star of the year

To be chosen is to:
a. be fat
b. be good
c. be picked

From the story you cannot tell:
a. how many home runs Babe Ruth hit
b. what team Babe played with
c. the color of Babe's baseball suit

The Runner Who Couldn't Walk

Wilma **Rudolph** didn't start out as a winner. She had seventeen brothers and sisters. Her family was very poor. When Wilma was four years old she became very sick. She couldn't walk anymore. But Wilma knew she would walk again. Slowly and painfully she began to walk. It was hard work.

By the time she reached high school, Wilma could walk and run. She played basketball and ran track. Because she was such a great runner, she got to go to **college**. In 1960, Wilma won three gold medals in the **Olympic** Games. She was named "Athlete of the Year".

After the Olympics, Wilma entered and won many other track meets. Wilma is no longer entering meets herself. She helps other girls who want to be track stars.

1. **The main idea of this story is:**
   a. Sometimes people can't walk.
   b. Wilma Rudolph is a coach.
   c. Wilma Rudolph became a great track star.

2. **Wilma:**
   a. owns a store
   b. helps other people who want to run
   c. teaches reading

3. **Wilma won:**
   a. a blue ribbon
   b. a new car
   c. gold medals

4. **Track is a sport in which you:**
   a. swim
   b. run as fast as you can
   c. race cars

5. **By learning to walk and run again, Wilma showed:**
   a. She was brave.
   b. She was silly.
   c. She was lazy.

Music for Everyone

Arthur **Fiedler** was a fine conductor. He started out by playing the **violin** in orchestras. His name even means "fiddler". In 1930 he was made conductor of the Boston Pops Orchestra. He conducted **concerts** until his death in 1979 at the age of 84.

Arthur Fiedler was different from other conductors. He knew that many people didn't like "serious" music. So Arthur decided to play the kind of music everyone would like. He played dance music and rock. He played the songs of the Beatles. He played music from shows and movies. Soon Arthur's music was even on TV. His program was called, "Evening at the Pops".

Arthur wanted people to buy his records, too. On the record covers he often dressed in costumes. Once he was Santa Claus. Another time he was Yankee Doodle Dandy. Arthur Fiedler said that all he wanted to do was to give people a good time.

1. **The main idea of this story is:**
   a. about orchestras
   b. about Arthur Fiedler
   c. about dance music

2. **Arthur Fiedler conducted:**
   a. trains
   b. music that many people liked
   c. only violin music

3. **Arthur's orchestra was called:**
   a. The Boston Pops
   b. The Boston Bulldogs
   c. The Boston Tea Party

4. **During a <u>concert</u>:**
   a. You see a movie.
   b. A team plays football.
   c. You listen to people playing or singing music.

5. **You can tell that:**
   a. Arthur Fiedler hated music.
   b. Arthur knew what people liked.
   c. Arthur was born in 1950.

Name _____   Date _____

"What's Up, Doc?"

Bugs Bunny runs across the screen. Elmer Fudd is chasing him. "Come back here, Wabbit!" Bugs answers, "Sorry, Doc, but I don't feel like being your dinner." In the next **cartoon**, Daffy Duck is in trouble as usual.

If you close your eyes, you know who each cartoon star is. Each of their voices is different. But guess what? All these voices were done by one man.

Mel Blanc was the voice of the Roadrunner, Wiley **Coyote** and many other cartoon **favorites**. You never saw Mel's face. But the voices he did were famous all over the world.

1. **The main idea of this story is:**
   a. how cartoons are made
   b. the many voices of Mel Blanc
   c. a famous rabbit

2. **Elmer likes to:**
   a. run after Bugs Bunny
   b. catch chickens
   c. play tennis

3. **Mel Blanc was the voice of:**
   a. Superman
   b. Daffy Duck
   c. the president

4. **In this story, a <u>screen</u> is:**
   a. what movies and TV are shown on
   b. something that keeps the bugs out
   c. a loud noise

5. **Mel Blanc probably:**
   a. plays the piano
   b. doesn't like insects
   c. liked his job

FS-32045 Reading

Name _____ Date _____

A Trip Around the World

In 1965, **Robin Graham** began his trip around the world. He was going to travel in a sailboat called the **Dove**. Robin was only sixteen years old.

Robin's father had helped him get ready for the trip. His father had also taught him to sail. But now Robin was all alone. Sometimes the trip seemed easy. The sun was shining. There was just enough wind to sail the boat. But sometimes there were bad storms. It rained for hours. Big waves splashed on the boat. During one big storm, part of the boat broke. Robin fell into the ocean and almost drowned. He pulled himself back onto the boat just in time.

In 1971, Robin finished his trip. He had sailed over 30,000 miles. He had met interesting people all over the world. He had seen strange fish, whales and seals. It had been a great adventure.

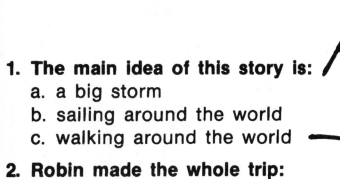

1. **The main idea of this story is:**
   a. a big storm
   b. sailing around the world
   c. walking around the world

2. **Robin made the whole trip:**
   a. by himself
   b. with his father
   c. with some friends

3. **What was the name of Robin's boat?**
   a. the Whale
   b. the Sea
   c. the Dove

4. **Just in time means:**
   a. before it is too late
   b. what time it is
   c. trying to be on time

5. **One reason it took Robin five years to make his trip probably was:**
   a. He stopped in many different places.
   b. He was lazy.
   c. He didn't like sailing.

Up, Up and Away!

On August 28, 1978, a balloon landed in a wheat field in **France**. When three men got out of the balloon's basket, people began cheering. The three men had just crossed the ocean in a balloon. They had traveled 3,100 miles. No one else had ever done this. The men's names were **Ben Abruzzo**, **Max Anderson** and **Larry Newman**.

The balloon was as high as a tall building. The men took along a boat in case something went wrong. Sometimes it got very cold high up in the air. They wore long underwear and had a little heater to keep warm. Once ice formed on the balloon. The big balloon began to go down. It looked like they might need the boat. But the sun melted the ice. The balloon rose up again. After five days the men finally reached land.

1. The main idea of this story is:
   a. Three men cross the ocean in a balloon.
   b. Three men cross the ocean in an airplane.
   c. One man takes a balloon around the world.

2. The three men were the first people to:
   a. cross the ocean in a balloon
   b. sail around the world
   c. take a balloon up in the air

3. How many miles did the balloon travel?
   a. 310 miles
   b. 3,000 miles
   c. 3,100 miles

4. In this story <u>in case</u> means:
   a. something you put things in
   b. if something should happen
   c. another way to travel

5. If the ice had not melted, the balloon might have:
   a. become very light
   b. sunk into the ocean
   c. changed colors

The Big Race

Antarctica is the coldest place on Earth. It is always covered with snow and ice. The South Pole is in the middle of Antarctica.

Until 1911, no one had ever traveled to the South Pole. However, **Robert Scott** decided he wanted to be the first one there. In 1910, Scott got on a ship for Antarctica. Just before he left, he received a letter from **Roald Amundsen.** The letter said, "Heading South". Amundsen was trying to beat Scott to the South Pole.

Amundsen arrived in Antarctica in 1911. On October 20, 1911, he set out for the South Pole by dog sled. Twelve days later, Scott set out for the South Pole. But he was too late. He was not able to catch up with Amundsen. On December 14 Amundsen reached the South Pole. He had won the race.

1. **The main idea of this story is:**
   a. Antarctica is a very cold place.
   b. Two men raced to the South Pole.
   c. Visiting the South Pole in the summer is fun.

2. **Roald Amundsen traveled over sea and _____ to reach the South Pole.**
   a. air
   b. water
   c. land

3. **Who reached the South Pole first?**
   a. Roald Amundsen
   b. Robert Scott
   c. Wild Bill Hickok

4. **To** <u>set out</u> **means:**
   a. to begin traveling
   b. to put something down
   c. to give something away

5. **One animal that might live at the South Pole is a:**
   a. seal
   b. camel
   c. lizard

FS-32045 Reading

Name _____ Date _____

The Man Who Loves Adventure

Naomi Uemura is a hero in Japan. But he is almost never there. Naomi loves travel and adventure. His biggest adventure so far has been his trip to the North Pole.

In 1978 Naomi began his trip by land to the North Pole. He traveled by dog sled. Naomi wore bearskin pants, fur mittens and heavy boots. There were many big snowstorms along the way. Sometimes the trail was blocked by small hills of ice. Then Naomi had to cut through the ice.

Once a polar bear visited his camp. Naomi pretended he was sleeping. The bear ate most of Naomi's food and ripped his tent. An airplane dropped more food for Naomi. Then, one of his dogs had puppies. Naomi sent the mother and puppies back and got more dogs. After 54 days Naomi reached the North Pole. He was the first man to make the trip alone.

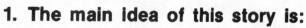

1. **The main idea of this story is:**
   a. A man travels to the North Pole alone.
   b. A polar bear eats all the food.
   c. A dog had puppies.

2. **On his trip, Naomi wore:**
   a. a bathing suit
   b. warm clothing
   c. light clothing

3. **What is the name of Naomi's country?**
   a. United States
   b. Japan
   c. England

4. **The word <u>ripped</u> means:**
   a. hurt
   b. made
   c. tore into pieces

5. **It is probably very ____ at the North Pole.**
   a. cold
   b. warm
   c. dry

FS-32045 Readin

Clara Barton was a great American woman who devoted her life to helping others. She founded the American Red Cross, a group which still helps millions of people.

During the Civil War she carried supplies to soldiers and nursed the wounded men. She was called the Angel of the Battlefield. At first the American government didn't help her, but later they realized how important she was.

She realized that the Red Cross could help people other than soldiers. Many of our people have been helped in time of emergency by the Red Cross. People need help during a disaster such as a flood.

Clara Barton took part in many kinds of **charitable** (volunteer) work. She wrote books and did patriotic work too.

The best title for this article is:
a. Mrs. Clara Barton
b. A Helpful Citizen
c. Clara Barton, a Great American
d. Helping Others

During the Civil War, Clara Barton was:
a. an American officer
b. a soldier
c. a nurse
d. a housewife

We will always remember that she began the:
a. Red Cross
b. nursing homes
c. Civil War
d. patriotic clubs

4. At first the American government:
a. encouraged her
b. wouldn't let her help
c. paid her
d. didn't realize her value

5. The word volunteer means:
a. a mother
b. a good person
c. someone who helps without pay
d. a nurse

6. Another happening much like the disaster mentioned in the story is:
a. an earthquake
b. rain
c. a vacation
d. a holiday

Name _____ Date _____

The Case of the Secret Valentine's Card

Rhoda was always being teased about being fat. She really was trying to stay on her diet. She ate her carrot sticks and dreamed of sweeter treats. "Hey, Rhoda, wake up," said Pauline at the lunch table. "Oh," sighed Rhoda, "I was thinking about a double dip of bubble gum ice cream." Pauline, Alice and Cindy laughed. Rhoda and Pauline left and went to their class. Everyone passed out their Valentine's cards. Rhoda almost cried when she read: Rhoda loves ice cream of bubble gum. It satisfies her fat tum-tum. Rhoda knew who sent it to her.

Whodunit and how did she know?_____

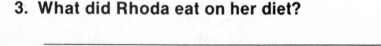

_____

1. **The main idea of this story is:**
   a. an ice cream treat
   b. a big bubble
   c. a mean poem

2. **Rhoda wanted _____ scoops of ice cream.**
   a. one
   b. two
   c. three

3. **What did Rhoda eat on her diet?**

   _____

4. **You can tell that Rhoda didn't like:**
   a. ice cream   b. her friends   c. being fat

5. **What holiday was it?**
   a. Christmas
   b. New Year's Day
   c. Valentine's Day

6. **Diet means:**
   a. eating certain foods
   b. being thin
   c. sending holiday cards

Brainwork! Think about the question and answer it on the back.
What should Rhoda say to the person who sent her the card?

48   FS-32045 Reading

esse James (1847-1882) was a bandit. He robbed banks and trains in Missouri and earby states.

He joined forces with his brother and several other men. The **band** of eight men tried o rob a bank at Northfield, Minnesota in 1876. Citizens fought them off, killing three .nd capturing three others. Only Jesse and his brother Frank escaped.

In 1881 the governor of Missouri offered a $5,000 reward for either brother. During that ear Jesse moved to St. Joseph, Missouri, where he posed as a cattle buyer and called imself Tom Howard. In the end he was shot by Robert Ford, a traitor from his own band.

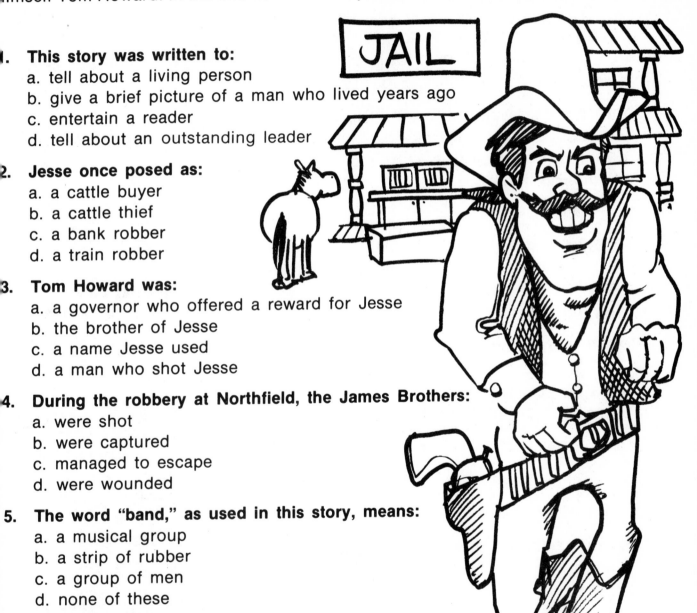

1. **This story was written to:**
   a. tell about a living person
   b. give a brief picture of a man who lived years ago
   c. entertain a reader
   d. tell about an outstanding leader

2. **Jesse once posed as:**
   a. a cattle buyer
   b. a cattle thief
   c. a bank robber
   d. a train robber

3. **Tom Howard was:**
   a. a governor who offered a reward for Jesse
   b. the brother of Jesse
   c. a name Jesse used
   d. a man who shot Jesse

4. **During the robbery at Northfield, the James Brothers:**
   a. were shot
   b. were captured
   c. managed to escape
   d. were wounded

5. **The word "band," as used in this story, means:**
   a. a musical group
   b. a strip of rubber
   c. a group of men
   d. none of these

6. **We can assume Jesse died:**
   a. in prison in 1882
   b. during a robbery
   c. from a shot fired by one of his own men in 1882
   d. of old age

 FS-32045 Reading

 # Rolling on Wheels

Everyone is roller skating! People skate on sidewalks and in parks. Mothers skate to the market and children skate to school. One man even skates 20 miles to work every day. Some people like to listen to music when they skate. They wear radios that fit over their ears. Other people like to wear fancy clothes when they skate.

People learn to dance or do tricks on skates. Some people can leap over lines of trash cans. Other people can skate backwards. **Champion** skaters often enter racing or dancing contests.

There are many different kinds of skates. The older skates had wood or metal wheels. Today most skates have big **rubber** wheels. If you feel tired you can even buy skates with motors. Then, just stand up and let the skates roll you home!

1. The main idea of this story is:
   a. People use skates in many different ways.
   b. Skating backwards is fun.
   c. People don't enjoy skating.

2. Skaters can enter:
   a. cooking contests
   b. beauty contests
   c. skating contests

3. Today most skate wheels are made of:
   a. wood
   b. rubber
   c. metal

4. Champion skaters are:
   a. losers
   b. scared
   c. winners

5. If you go too fast on skates you may:
   a. start flying
   b. fall down
   c. climb up a tree

FS-32045 Reading

Name _____ Date _____

Jumps and Bumps

It's the day of the big motorcycle race. The racers are dressed in **leather** pants, **jackets**, boots and gloves. They all wear safety **helmets**.

It will be a hard race. The race will be held on a dirt track. The track has two jumps and some big mud puddles.

What a lot of noise! The engines have started up. The racers are lined up at the starting line. The race begins! The track has a lot of bumps in it. One man's motorcycle turns over but he is all right. There's the first jump. A racer takes the jump. His cycle lifts off the ground and then lands on its back wheel.

Another motorcycle gets stuck in the mud and its wheels begin to spin. Some racers drop out of the race. The winner is covered with mud and dust. But he is very happy.

1. **The main idea of this story is:**
   a. Racers keep their clothes very clean.
   b. Motorcycle racing is an exciting sport.
   c. Motorcycle racers go to school.

2. **Motorcycle engines are:**
   a. very quiet
   b. very small
   c. very noisy

3. **All motorcycle racers wear:**
   a. safety helmets
   b. white shoes
   c. baseball caps

4. **The word jacket means:**
   a. shirt
   b. tie
   c. short coat

5. **Motorcycle racers must be careful:**
   a. not to make too much noise
   b. not to turn over their cycles
   c. to stay clean

FS-32045 Reading

Faster and Faster

The boy stood at the top of the hill. It looked like a long way down to the bottom. He put on his **helmet, knee** pads and **elbow** pads. He placed one foot on his skateboard and pushed off with the other foot. Suddenly, he saw some bumps in the middle of the road. He leaned to the right and the skateboard moved to the right. He just missed the bumps. He began going faster and faster. Soon he was going over 30 miles an hour. He reached the bottom. He turned his board to the side and stopped.

Skateboards have four small wheels. Boards are made of **plastic**, metal or wood. Good skateboard riders can do many tricks. They skate in special parks, safe streets or on sidewalks. Some skateboard riders even skate up the walls of empty swimming pools!

1. **The main idea of this story is:**
   a. Always put pads on your skateboards.
   b Skateboard riding is an exciting sport.
   c. Skateboard riders move very slowly.

2. **If you lean to the left on a skateboard you will go:**
   a. to the left
   b. to the right
   c. around in a circle

3. **How many wheels does a skateboard have?**
   a. one
   b. four
   c. three

4. **A <u>helmet</u> is something:**
   a you put on your head
   b. you throw in the air
   c. you feed to the animals

5. **Skateboard riders wear pads so they:**
   a. bump into a lot of people
   b. won't hurt themselves when they fall
   c. can jump high in the air

FS-32045 Readin

Welcome to the Wild West

This is just like the Wild West. Today is the opening of the rodeo. Cowboys and cowgirls have come from all over to enter the contests. During the year they work on ranches. They rope cattle and ride horses all day. Once a year they can show off these **skills** at the rodeo.

The first contest is **bronc** riding. A bronc is a wild horse. One horse is called Fireball. He looks very mean. The cowboy gets on Fireball and tries to hang on. The horse kicks his legs in the air. He jumps up and down. But the cowboy stays on Fireball for ten seconds. He wins the contest.

Now it's time for the barrel race. Sue Green rides her horse around three barrels. She doesn't knock down any barrels. Some of the other cowgirls do knock down barrels. Sue is the winner.

It has been an exciting day. Tomorrow the cowboys and cowgirls will be headed back to their ranches.

1. **The main idea of this story is:**
   a A rodeo is made up of different contests.
   b. Only cowboys can enter rodeos.
   c. There are lions and tigers at rodeos.

2. **Cowgirls and cowboys learn to rope and ride:**
   a. at the beach
   b on ranches
   c. in the jungle

3. **How many barrels are there in a barrel race?**
   a three
   b. two
   c. four

4. **A bronc is:**
   a. a bull
   b. a wild horse
   c. a wild cow

5. **A cowboy or cowgirl should be:**
   a. very funny
   b. a good rider
   c. a fast runner

Name _____ Date _____

 **A Day at the Circus**

The band begins to play. It's time for the circus! First there is a big parade around the ring. Women in beautiful costumes ride on elephants. Next, a clown drives a little car around the ring. He stops the car and out come 20 clowns!

The parade ends and the show begins. First, the horseback rider leaps into the air and lands on her horse. Then, the animal trainer comes out. He walks into a cage filled with lions and tigers. The lions and tigers growl and show their teeth. But the animal trainer is not afraid. He waves a small stick in the air. The animals jump onto little **stools**.

Finally, a man walks across the high wire. He is very high up in the air. The wire begins to shake. It looks like he will fall. He walks to the end of the wire and jumps safely onto the **platform**. Everyone claps their hands. What a wonderful show!

1. The main idea of this story is:
   a. going to the circus
   b. going to the zoo
   c. watching a big parade

2. The circus has:
   a. many different things to see
   b. no animals in the show
   c. airplanes

3. Who works with the lions and tigers?
   a. the clowns
   b. the animal trainer
   c. the man on the high wire

4. The word <u>platform</u> means:
   a. a big table
   b. the end of a wire
   c. a flat stage above the ground

5. Animal trainers probably:
   a. like working with animals
   b. are afraid of animals
   c. want to become clowns

FS-32045 Readir

A Town for Little People

Madurodam in **Holland** looks like many other towns. It has houses, roads, parks and an airport. The street lights turn on at night. Cars and buses move along the highways. There is a big traffic jam downtown. In the park, the merry-go-round turns round and round. But there is something very different about this city. Many of the buildings are shorter than a person's leg. The street lights are only as tall as pencils standing on end. And the people are three inches tall.

Of course the people are only little dolls. Everything in Madurodam is much smaller than in real life. The little buildings are **models** of real buildings in Holland. Since Madurodam was first built, over 15 million people have visited it. Parents enjoy the tiny city as much as their children.

1. **The main idea of this story is:**
   a. a town for giants
   b. people are three inches tall
   c. a town where everything is little

2. **Madurodam is different than other cities in:**
   a. size
   b. color
   c. number of buildings

3. **In what country is Madurodam?**
   a. Holland
   b. England
   c. the United States

4. **The word <u>model</u> means:**
   a. a new kind of food
   b. a small copy of something
   c. a new way to make things

5. **A car in Madurodam might be the size of:**
   a. a desk
   b. a horse
   c. an apple

A Statue for Freedom

The **Statue** of **Liberty** stands in New York Harbor. It is known all over the world. It is a statue of a beautiful woman. She wears a crown on her head. But she is not a queen. In one hand she holds a book of law. In the other hand she holds a light. At night the light can be seen from far away.

France gave the statue to the United States in 1884. It is one of the largest statues ever made. The statue is 151 feet tall. It weighs 450,000 pounds. There is a staircase leading to the top of its crown. From the top, visitors can see the harbor and New York City. The Statue of Liberty stands for freedom. It is the first thing many people see when they enter the United States. It means they have come to a free country.

1. The main idea of this story is:
   a. boats in the harbor
   b. a big boat
   c. facts about a famous statue

2. The Statue of Liberty is:
   a. very heavy
   b. in England
   c. in the middle of the desert

3. Who gave the Statue of Liberty to the United States?
   a. Soviet Union
   b. France
   c. England

4. The word <u>liberty</u> means:
   a. to be free
   b. to buy something
   c. to go to the movies

5. The Statue of Liberty is probably made of:
   a. paper
   b. feathers
   c. metal

The Magic Kingdom

The Jones family was going to **Disneyland**. Sara Jones was very excited. "I hope I see Mickey Mouse and Donald Duck," she said.

When they arrived, Sara thought Disneyland looked like a magic **kingdom**. There was a beautiful castle in the middle of the park. And there were her friends, Mickey and Donald, waving at her.

First Sara went on the Jungle Boat Ride. She saw elephants, lions and zebras. Then Sara went on the Submarine Ride. It went under the water. A big sea **monster** was swimming in the water. The monster looked like it was smiling.

There were so many things to do. There were train rides and a merry-go-round. One exciting ride was the **Matterhorn**. Sara got into a little car on tracks. It went up and down the mountain very fast. At night, fireworks went off in the park. It was the end of a wonderful day.

1. **The main idea of this story is:**
   a. There are monsters in Disneyland.
   b. Mickey Mouse lives in Disneyland.
   c. There are many things to do in Disneyland.

2. **The sea monster seemed:**
   a. friendly
   b. angry
   c. scary

3. **The first ride Sara rode was:**
   a. the Submarine Ride
   b. the Jungle Boat Ride
   c. the Spaceship Ride

4. **A <u>kingdom</u> is:**
   a. a big zoo
   b. a house filled with people
   c. a country ruled by a king

5. **To see all of Disneyland, it would probably take:**
   a. a half hour
   b. one year
   c. all day

Name _____ Date _____

The President's House

Imagine you were president of the United States. You would meet important people from all over the world. Sometimes you would travel to different cities and talk to the American people. You would even be able to live in the White House.

The White House is painted all white on the outside. It was first built in 1800. But the first building burned down. The White House was rebuilt in 1817. Since then, all the presidents have lived there. Each one has changed the White House a little. Today, the White House has 132 rooms. Some of the rooms are named after colors. There is a Red Room, a Blue Room and a Green Room. The dining room can seat 140 people. Imagine what your mother would say if you brought 140 people home for dinner!

1. **The main idea of this story is:**
   a. how to become a president
   b. about the White House
   c. building the White House

2. **The White House is:**
   a. less than 50 years old
   b. more than 150 years old
   c. 10 years old

3. **Some of the rooms are named after:**
   a. colors
   b. animals
   c. people

4. **In this story the word <u>seat</u> means:**
   a. a big pillow to sit on
   b. how many people can sit in a room
   c. sitting down at the same time

5. **Another person who might live in the White House is:**
   a. a rock star
   b. the President's wife
   c. the Queen of England

FS-32045 Readir

A Floating City

In **Venice, Italy,** children don't ride buses to school. They ride motor boats. enice is a city made up of 120 small islands. There are no roads in the city. ut there are waterways called **canals**. People use boats instead of cars or uses. Some people ride in long rowboats called **gondolas**. There are over 50 canals in the city. If people want to take a walk, they use the walkways long the canals. There are also 400 bridges which cross over the canals.

Venice is a very beautiful city. It has many old buildings. But it is not always safe place to live. Sometimes when it rains, the houses get filled with **water**. nd for a long time Venice was sinking a little every year. People were afraid at one day Venice would sink into the ocean. But the problem was solved nd the city was saved.

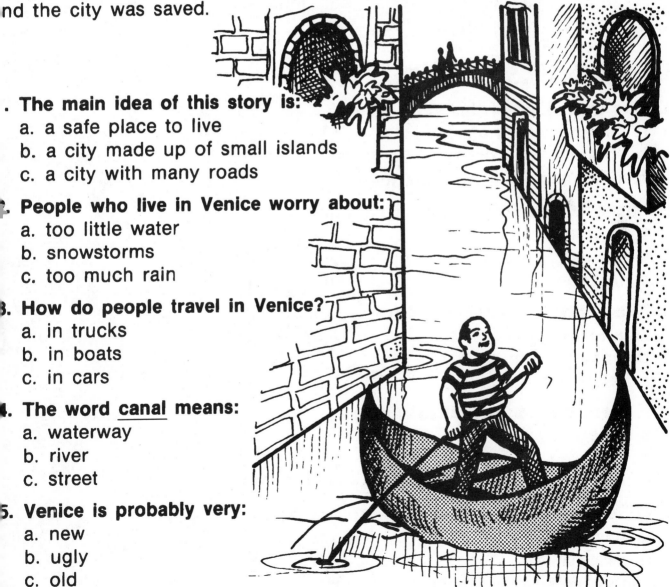

. **The main idea of this story is:**
   a. a safe place to live
   b. a city made up of small islands
   c. a city with many roads

. **People who live in Venice worry about:**
   a. too little water
   b. snowstorms
   c. too much rain

. **How do people travel in Venice?**
   a. in trucks
   b. in boats
   c. in cars

. **The word** <u>canal</u> **means:**
   a. waterway
   b. river
   c. street

. **Venice is probably very:**
   a. new
   b. ugly
   c. old

Where Animals Run Free

Most of us only see wild animals in the zoo. But in **Africa**, there is a specia[l] park just for wild animals. The park is called **Serengeti**. In Serengeti zebras buffalos, lions and elephants run free. There are also giraffes, wild dogs and monkeys in the park.

The animals like Serengeti because there is a lot of good grass to eat. The[ ] park also has many streams and lakes. Elephants fill their trunks with water from the streams and take baths. Monkeys play games and dig for bugs with sticks. Tall giraffes eat leaves from the treetops. Thousands of zebras gather in one place to eat grass.

There are also dangers in Serengeti. Lions hunt the zebras and buffalos. Large snakes creep through the grass. In Serengeti, each day is filled with adventure.

1. **The main idea of this story is:**
   a. Serengeti is a big zoo.
   b. There are no cages in Serengeti.
   c. Only people live in Serengeti.

2. **In the United States, most wild animals live:**
   a. in houses
   b. in parks
   c. in zoos

3. **The animals like Serengeti because there is:**
   a. a lot of grass to eat
   b. popcorn and soda
   c. television

4. **If there are <u>dangers</u>, then a place is:**
   a. safe
   b. fun
   c. not safe

5. **If Serengeti was a desert, it would probably:**
   a. have a lot of water
   b. be very cold
   c. not have many animals

FS-32045 Readin[g]

Boiling Water

In **Yellowstone Park**, creeks are filled with hot, bubbling water. A river in this park is cold on top and hot on the bottom. And there are holes in the ground that blow out steam. The steam holes are called **geysers**. The steam and heat comes from inside the earth. There are over 10,000 geysers and hot springs in Yellowstone.

The best known geyser is **Old Faithful**. Every 65 minutes it sprays out steam and hot water. It uses 10,000 gallons of water in four minutes. Sometimes the water spray is over 100 feet tall.

Geysers are very interesting, but they can also be very tricky. Once a man tried to wash his clothes in a geyser. He put his clothes and soap in it. Just then the geyser blew up. The man's clothes went flying in the air.

1. The main idea of this story is:
a. Wash your clothes every week.
b. Watch out for cold water.
c. Geysers do strange things.

2. Old Faithful goes off about once:
a. an hour
b. a day
c. a year

3. How many geysers are there in Yellowstone Park?
a. 1,000
b. more than 1,000
c. less than 1,000

4. In this story, <u>faithful</u> means:
a. to own something
b. to always do something on time
c. to have a lot of friends

5. Some geysers are probably:
a. very cold
b. found in zoos
c. hot enough to cook food

Rock Trees

Once there were tall trees standing in the **Petrified** Forest. The forest also had bushes, flowers and streams. But that was millions of years ago. Today the grass is gone and the land has become a desert. The trees have fallen down and lie on the ground. They look soft. But they are hard enough to break a saw. They can only be cut with special tools. The trees have turned to stone.

Many years ago a big flood knocked down many of the trees. They were buried in the mud. Then water with metal in it dripped into the trees. Slowly the trees turned to stone. The wind and rain uncovered them after thousands of years. Today there are only wood chips, tree stumps and logs in the forest. Some of the logs are 100 feet long. More logs may still be buried deep in the ground.

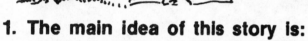

1. **The main idea of this story is:**
   a. Trees have turned to stone.
   b. There are many streams in the Petrified Forest.
   c. The trees in the Petrified Forest are easy to cut.

2. **Some of the logs in the forest are very:**
   a. soft
   b. good to eat
   c. long

3. **Today the Petrified Forest is a:**
   a. city
   b. desert
   c. farm

4. **A** <u>petrified</u> **tree is made of:**
   a. wood
   b. food
   c. stone

5. **From this story you can tell the trees are:**
   a. dead
   b. still growing
   c. green

FS-32045 Readin

Strange Stones

The **Carlsbad Caverns** are large caves deep under the ground. One of the caves is the largest in the world. It is big enough to cover fourteen football fields. The Carlsbad Caverns are very old. Animals lived in the caves over 200 million years ago. Today, only bats live there. At one time there were over eight million bats in the caves.

Every year many people visit the Carlsbad Caverns. In the caves there are big lights so people can see the **limestone** rocks. Some of the rocks look like animals or people. One rock is called Whale's Mouth. Another rock is called Three Little Monkeys. There is even a rock that looks like Santa Claus. The rocks were formed by dripping water. Some rocks hang from the ceiling. Other rocks rise up from the floor.

At the end of the walk, visitors eat in a lunchroom 754 feet under the ground.

1. **The main idea of this story is:**
   a. Some caves are very small.
   b. Carlsbad Caverns has interesting rocks.
   c. Carlsbad Caverns is a very dark place.

2. **Some of the caves in the Carlsbad Caverns are:**
   a. very light
   b. filled with snakes
   c. very large

3. **Animals lived in the caves over:**
   a. 200 million years ago
   b. 200 years ago
   c. 50 million years ago

4. **Limestone is a:**
   a. stone fruit
   b. kind of rock
   c. cold drink

5. **Since the caves are underground, you can guess that:**
   a. A lot of plants grow there.
   b. They are very dark.
   c. Birds fly around.

If you're thinking about ordering an extra paper to read during the evening, let me offer you a word of warning: Beware of Bruce! Bruce wanted to win a trip to camp, so I was more than glad to help him out by taking the newspaper.

The first night, Bruce whizzed by on his bike and tossed the paper over my fence. What aim! It landed in the garbage and I didn't find it for two days, yellowed and fading. The next day, our dog, Beetle, found the paper first and chewed it to shreds trying to get the rubber band off. On the third day, I got the paper all in one piece—right through the front window!

I hope Bruce goes to camp and gives up his paper route!

1. **The main idea of this story is:**

   a. a dangerous paper boy
   b. taking a trip to summer camp
   c. a newspaper fades in the garbage

2. **Bruce wanted to win**

   a. a contest by selling papers.
   b. a prize for feeding a dog.
   c. a bicycle to take to camp.

3. **Where did Bruce want to go on a trip?**

   a. to the mountains or a ranch
   b. to school or a zoo
   c. to the museum or a movie

4. **What does "beware" mean?**

   a. to be afraid
   b. to be disliked
   c. to be careful

5. **You might think Bruce**

   a. had never delivered papers before.
   b. didn't want to go to camp.
   c. liked riding his bike at night.

"Yesterday afternoon I brought a nice wood box down from the attic, and now it's gone. Quite a few things have been disappearing from this living room lately. Do you know what's happened, Davy?"

"I think the ghost that lives upstairs came down and took it back," Davy told his mother. "He likes certain things up there to make him feel at home. Maybe we should try to find an old table and chair to make him more comfortable when he's not out haunting houses. Come to think of it, I'll bet that ghost would like to have a television set, too. If we keep him happy, I just know that ghost will never bother you, Mom."

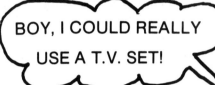

BOY, I COULD REALLY USE A T.V. SET!

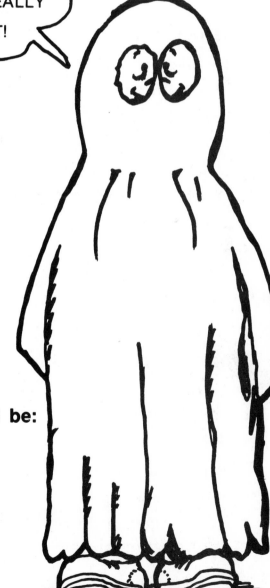

1. **The main idea of this story is:**

   a. a ghost comes to live with Davy
   b. a ghost that likes to feel at home
   c. a story of a haunted house

2. **Mother felt there was something**

   a. alive in the living room.
   b. terrible happening.
   c. mysterious going on.

3. **Where did the ghost live?**

   a. in a haunted house
   b. in the attic
   c. in Davy's room

4. **Another word for "disappearing" would be:**

   a. happening
   b. vanishing
   c. describing

5. **You might think that the ghost was:**

   a. moving out of the house
   b. Davy himself
   c. a thief

I have a younger brother who could easily win the "Pest Of The Year Award". When Mark was four years old, he was just your average, run-of-the-mill pest. Today, three years later, he has developed into a first-class trouble maker. One evening, I found Mark outside collecting insects in a jar. "What are you doing, Mark?"

"I'm catching these for you to add to your bug collection, Wendy."

"Isn't that thoughtful," I said to myself. But I should have known better. A few hours later, I walked into my room and there sitting in my bookcase were fifteen grasshoppers, grinning from ear to ear. They were so full from having gulped down my entire bug collection, all they could do was hiccup. No more favors, please!

1. **The main idea of this story is:**

    a. a pest "bugs" his sister
    b. collecting insects at night in the garden
    c. the grasshopper's dinner feast

2. **Bug collecting can be a favorite hobby or a**

    a. waste of time.
    b. part of science.
    c. dinner party.

3. **How old is Mark in the story?**

    a. 4 years old
    b. 7 years old
    c. you can't tell

4. **What is another good word for "gulped"?**

    a. choked
    b. swallowed
    c. tasted

5. **The jar Mark used probably**

    a. wasn't very large.
    b. didn't have a lid on it.
    c. had peanut butter in it.

"Uh-oh, I think my hamster escaped! I've got to find him."

"Joey, I told you not to bring that animal in here! Pets aren't allowed in rocery stores," mother scolded him.

"I see his tail," Joey shouted, shoving his hand into a stack of paper owels. But the hamster scampered away and towels rolled everywhere. "I ee two ears sticking up between those cans. I'll get him now," Joey yelled limbing up on a shelf. Down clattered eighteen cans of carrots, ten cans of eets and eight cans of green beans.

Just then the store owner dashed over to Joey's mother. "From now on, I on't think I'll allow children in my store. They are more dangerous than nimals!"

The main idea of this story is:

a. children can be dangerous too
b. paper towels rolling off shelves
c. a hamster hides from mother

Joey knocked over

a. cans of fruit.
b. cans of vegetables.
c. cans of soup.

What was Joey trying to do?

a. get a roll of paper towels
b. capture his hamster
c. ruin the store

Paper towels come on a "roll". Another kind of "role" is

a. a part in a play.
b. a coffee-cake.
c. a bouncing ball.

5. **From the story you cannot tell if**

a. Joey caught the hamster.
b. towels spilled everywhere.
c. mother was angry at Joey.

For two years I worked very hard learning to be a good speller, harder than you can imagine! I studied twenty new words every week for about two hours, and most of the time I got "A"s on my tests. I didn't think there was a single word I couldn't spell by sounding out the letters and knowing a few other secrets, like "i before e except after c".

Yesterday we had a surprise test. When I saw my paper today, I was as mad as a bumblebee! I spelled "photograph"—"fotograf", "knife"—"nife" and "cough"—"cof". This doesn't make any sense to me at all. The person who wrote the dictionary should come to school with me and learn how to spell!

SURE I CAN SPELL "EMPTY"!

IT'S SPELLED "M, T"!

1. **The main idea of this story is:**

   a. students studying for a spelling test
   b. spelling doesn't make any sense
   c. rewriting a dictionary

2. **Some letters in a word**

   a. are not in the alphabet.
   b. have three different sounds.
   c. make no sound or different sounds.

3. **One thing the story doesn't tell is:**

   a. how to spell photograph
   b. how many words were studied
   c. how everyone else did on the test

4. **"To make sense" means to "be clear".
   Another kind of sense is:**

   a. the sense of taste
   b. the sense of action
   c. the sense of dictionary

5. **You can guess that the person in the story**

   a. did not have a good memory.
   b. was confused by silent letters and odd spelling.
   c. wanted to try again and take another test.

FS-32045 Readin

As I ran upstairs to bed, I heard Mom say, "Hang your uniform in the closet." It was the night before the big game and I really wanted to win. I was very tired, so I dropped my clothes over a chair and climbed quickly into bed. I was soon asleep.

In the morning I dressed quickly. One sock was missing. Who could have taken my sock? I was so sure I had put everything on the chair. I looked everywhere. I had to play the big game with only one team sock. We lost the game.

When I got home I saw a **touch** of blue and gold in Skipper's box. Skipper had taken my sock. I thought about it for a while. Skipper couldn't reach the clothes on my chair. How did my dog get my sock?

1. **The most interesting title for this story is:**
   a. Why You Should Hang Up Your Clothes
   b. Be Prepared
   c. The Big Game
   d. The Mystery of the Missing Sock

2. **The story took place:**
   a. before a big game
   b. in the morning
   c. at night
   d. at several times

3. **The person in the story didn't hang up his clothes because:**
   a. he was in a hurry to leave
   b. he was tired
   c. he was too excited
   d. he didn't know how

4. **The reason his team lost the game was:**
   a. he didn't have a sock
   b. he couldn't play without his whole uniform
   c. the other team was really great
   d. the story doesn't say

5. **The word "touch," in the story means:**
   a. put one's finger on
   b. tap lightly
   c. a small amount
   d. a color

6. **Most likely the dog got the sock because:**
   a. he pulled it off the chair
   b. someone gave it to him
   c. it had fallen on the floor
   d. a larger dog found it first

Name _____

Although there seem to be **countless** stars in the sky, there are even more differen
kinds of insects. Scientists have found more than 800,000 kinds of insects, but
authorities believe there may be as many as 4,000,000 species.

Insects live nearly everywhere they can find food. It is hard to find food in the ocean
therefore very few insects are found there.

The insect plays a most important part in our lives because he eats so much and i
getting food, he aids man. The honey-bee is an example of helpfulness.

Other insects are harmful. They bite men and destroy millions of dollars in crops eac
year.

1. **The best title for this story is:**
   a. Hundreds of Insects
   b. Interesting Insects
   c. How Insects Help Us
   d. How Insects Hurt Us

2. **Scientists have identified more than:**
   a. 4 million species of insects
   b. several species of insects
   c. 800,000 kinds of insects
   d. only a few species

3. **Few insects live in the oceans because:**
   a. it is too wet there
   b. they can't fly underwater
   c. they find little food there
   d. they can't do much damage there

4. **Insects are:**
   a. helpful
   b. harmful
   c. large
   d. both A and B

5. **The word "countless" means:**
   a. less than we can count
   b. countable
   c. more than we can count
   d. not too many

6. **Since some insects are harmful:**
   a. insects should be killed
   b. harmful insects need to be destroyed or controlled as much as possible
   c. we should get more helpful insects
   d. we don't need any insects

FS-32045 Readin

Name _____

A soapbox derby is a coasting race for small motorless racing cars. The race was named soapbox because sometimes the cars are made from wooden soapboxes.

The contestants are kids between the ages of 11 and 15. They build the racing cars. There are rules which govern the size and **weight** of the racer, how it is built and how much it can cost.

There are local races. The winners of these races then attend the All-American and International Soapbox Derby in Akron, Ohio. A college scholarship is offered to the winner of these final contests.

People from the United States, Canada, South America and Europe enter the Derby. Thousands of spectators view the race each year.

1. **The best title for this story is:**
   a. The Soapbox Derby
   b. Racing
   c. Children's Racing Derby
   d. A Racing Contest

2. **In the word "motorless," the suffix less means:**
   a. not as much
   b. little
   c. without a
   d. none of these

3. **You may spend _____ on the car you build:**
   a. any amount
   b. an amount stated in the rules
   c. a large amount
   d. a small amount

4. **The final races are held in:**
   a. Europe
   b. South America
   c. Canada
   d. none of these

5. **The word "weight" means:**
   a. heaviness
   b. amount
   c. pause a while
   d. stop

6. **We can assume that many people enjoy the Derbies because the article says:**
   a. everyone watches it
   b. millions of people watch it
   c. thousands of people see it
   d. only a few attend the Derby

FS-32045 Reading

The kangaroo rat is a tiny animal that jumps around like a kangaroo. The rat can leap on his powerful hind legs. His tail is about as long as his body.

He comes out at night to search for food. His eyes are large and he can see well in the dark.

Kangaroo rats have silky fur of yellow or brown on the upper parts of their bodies and white underparts. They can **stuff** food into fur-lined pouches on the outside of their cheeks. They do not need to drink water. They get water from inside themselves when their food combines with the oxygen they breathe.

These rats live in the deserts of the southwestern United States.

1. **The best title for this story is:**
   a. Small animals
   b. The Kangaroo Rat
   c. How Kangaroos Get Water
   d. How a Kangaroo Looks

2. **These rats are able to hunt for food at night because:**
   a. they can see well in the dark
   b. they know where to look
   c. they can smell food
   d. their eyes are too large

3. **These rats may be:**
   a. yellow and white
   b. brown and white
   c. either A and B
   d. brown and yellow

4. **If a kangaroo rat is about 15 inches including the tail, the tail is about:**
   a. 9 inches long
   b. 3 or 4 inches long
   c. about 7½ inches long
   d. there is no way to guess

5. **In this article, the word "stuff" means:**
   a. junk
   b. food
   c. place or put
   d. carry

6. **These rats probably survive well in desert areas because:**
   a. they have always lived there
   b. they don't need water
   c. it is nice and warm there
   d. people won't go there to hunt

FS-32045 Reading

Some fish are able to **inflate** their bodies like balloons. The common name of such a
sh is "puffer fish" or "swell fish." Some common puffers live along the Atlantic coast,
hile others live in tropical waters.

Most of the time the puffer looks like an ordinary fish with a large head and mouth that
ppears to have teeth sticking out. When the fish is disturbed, it inflates its stomach with
ir. After it is inflated, it floats belly upward on the surface of water until the danger has
assed. It may blow itself to twice its normal size.

The name "puffer" may be confused with the word "puffin," which is actually an
dd-looking bird that lives in the Arctic.

The two best titles for this story are:
a. Inflatable Fish
b. Puffins
c. Puffer Fish
d. Unusual Animals

Generally the fish inflates itself when:
a. it senses danger
b. it is happy
c. it is disturbed
d. both A and C

When inflated, the fish is:
a. two times as big as usual
b. smaller
c. three times larger than usual
d. many times larger than usual

The puffin is a:
a. fish
b. a bird
c. another name for puffer
d. none of these

The word "swell" is a name that indicates a fish that:
a. is great
b. can enlarge itself
c. is really super
d. is in rising swirls of water

6. **From the way the word "inflate" is used in the story we can guess it means:**
a. a balloon
b. take in air
c. blows out
d. moves

FS-32045 Reading

One of the greediest eaters and killers among sea animals is the shark. Sharks live in all **parts** of the sea, but they seem to prefer warm areas. They may grow to be over 40 feet long. Their bodies are covered with scales which give the skin a rough feeling much like sandpaper. Although many sharks have rows of long, sharp teeth, others have broad, flat teeth. Sharks can swim rapidly and may follow ships for days waiting for food to be thrown overboard.

The largest shark, the whale shark, is harmless to man. It is often over 50 feet long but feeds only on small sea animals and plants. This is the largest known fish. The whale, which is larger, is not a fish. It is a mammal.

Sharks are used by man for making glue, fertilizer, cod-liver oil, leather and food.

1. **The best title for this story is:**
    a. The Many Uses of Sharks
    b. Sharks
    c. Fish of Many Kinds
    d. The Largest Shark

2. **The largest known fish is:**
    a. a whale
    b. any shark
    c. the whale shark
    d. the article doesn't say

3. **Sharks prefer areas that are:**
    a. warm
    b. near people
    c. near boats
    d. near other fish

4. **The largest shark often:**
    a. eats people
    b. is over 50 feet long
    c. eats large sea animals and plants
    d. swims faster than ships

5. **In this article, the word "parts" means:**
    a. pieces
    b. separates with a comb
    c. sections
    d. bodies

6. **Sharks can be used for:**
    a. food
    b. leather
    c. fertilizer
    d. all of these

FS-32045 Reading

Name _____

Small squirrels that can glide through the air are called flying squirrels. These squirrels live in the forests of Asia, Europe and North America.

A fold of skin on each side of the squirrel's body connects the front and back legs. When he stretches out his front and back legs, the skin makes gliding wings. As it glides from tree to tree, the squirrel uses its broad flat tail to guide its flight. He can cover from 50 to 100 feet in a leap, but generally covers about 50 to 60 feet.

These squirrels are only 8 to 12 inches long including their tails. They live in the hollows of trees and hunt for food only at night. Other squirrels hunt **by** day. They eat a variety of things including berries, bird's eggs, insect, nuts, young birds or dead animals.

1. **The main purpose of this story is to tell about:**
   a. squirrels
   b. small animals
   c. flying animals
   d. squirrels that seem to fly

2. **The "wings" of the squirrel are formed by:**
   a. the legs
   b. the arms
   c. folds of skin
   d. all of these together

3. **The "flight" is guided by:**
   a. the squirrel
   b. the wind direction
   c. the animal's tail
   d. the distance to travel

4. **The flying squirrel usually leaps about:**
   a. 100 feet
   b. over 75 feet
   c. 50 to 60 feet
   d. under 15 feet

5. **In the article, the word "by" means:**
   a. near
   b. past
   c. purchase
   d. during

6. **These animals are probably considered different from other squirrels because:**
   a. they seem to fly
   b. they hunt at night
   c. they are 8 to 12 inches long
   d. both A and B

FS-32045 Reading

Skin diving is another name for "free" diving. The diver goes underwater with no a
supply from which to breathe.

Skin divers explore the world beneath the surface of rivers, lakes or oceans. They ma
take pictures, hunt fish or just study nature. This type of diving is usually done fo
recreation.

Skin divers may also search for evidence in crimes or disasters, repair ships, or c
other important work under water. Since a skin diver can move around easily, he can c
jobs that would be difficult for a diver with a helmet and air hose.

Most skin divers wear face masks and rubber foot fins. They often use a snorkel, whic
is a tube that allows them to breathe underwater.

1. **The best title for this story is:**
    a. Life Under Water
    b. Going for a Swim
    c. The Art of Skin Diving
    d. Studying Fish

2. **The diver has no:**
    a. fins
    b. mask
    c. air supply
    d. camera

3. **A detective might hire a skin diver:**
    a. to find evidence
    b. to find a special fish
    c. to haul up a sunken ship
    d. to repair a boat

4. **It is easier for a skin diver to do some kinds of work than it would be for a diver with**
    a helmet because:
    a. he can stay underwater longer
    b. he takes up less space
    c. he isn't connected to cords and can move easily
    d. he doesn't charge as much

5. **The word "recreation" means:**
    a. work
    b. fun
    c. a park
    d. money

6. **One thing a skin diver must know is:**
    a. where a boat sank
    b. who will pay him
    c. how deep the water is
    d. how to swim

FS-32045 Readin

One day Jan was visiting her grandmother. Her grandmother had been cleaning drawers before Jan arrived and had left some of her favorite jewelry on the dresser. When Jan **saw** the jewelry, she decided to try on a bracelet.

Suddenly Grandmother called for her to come and eat some freshly baked cookies. She hurried downstairs and enjoyed the treat.

Later she went out to play with Pal, grandmother's dog. When she remembered the bracelet, she saw it was gone. She looked everywhere but she couldn't find it.

Jan was a very unhappy girl. She had taken something that wasn't her own. She knew she must tell Grandmother what happened. Grandmother said she would try to help.

1. **The best title for this story is:**
   a. A Happy Visit
   b. Grandmother's House
   c. Jan and Pal
   d. The Lost Bracelet

2. **Jan made a mistake when:**
   a. she tried on the bracelet without permission
   b. she went outside
   c. she played with the dog
   d. she ate too many cookies

3. **Jan was probably most unhappy because:**
   a. she had taken something that didn't belong to her
   b. she knew Grandmother would be angry
   c. she lost the bracelet
   d. the dog had taken the bracelet

4. **She knew the best thing she could do now is:**
   a. tell the truth and ask for help
   b. hunt some more
   c. buy a new bracelet
   d. cry

5. **In this story, the word "saw" means:**
   a. take the cover off
   b. see it through the grass
   c. found
   d. look for it

6. **The best rule to follow is:**
   a. put back things you take
   b. get permission before borrowing things
   c. don't lose things
   d. don't tell anyone if you lose something

Ohio has changed from a farm state to a state famous for big, busy cities.

It has an important steel center and factories which make glass and automobile part Great quantities of coal are **shipped** from Toledo, and Akron is the rubber city of t nation. Cincinnati makes soap, playing cards and machinery. The soil is rich and whe oats, corn, soybeans and tobacco are grown in Ohio. Eight U.S. presidents came from Ohio.

Ohio is called the "Buckeye State" because of the Buckeye leaves on many trees. It wa named after the Ohio River. Ohio means "beautiful river."

1. **The best title for this story is:**
   a. An Important State
   b. Ohio, An Important State
   c. A State of Large Cities
   b. "Beautiful River"

2. **After reading the article we know that:**
   a. Ohio has many farms
   b. Ohio has many rivers that are beautiful
   c. Ohio has fewer farms than it had in the past.
   d. Ohio is the birthplace of most presidents

3. **Ohio is called the "Buckeye State" because:**
   a. of the Buckeye leaves on the trees
   b. many buckeye peas grow there
   c. it was named after a man
   d. it is overrun with buckeyes

4. **Akron is important as a center for:**
   a. soap
   b. wheat, oats and corn
   c. rubber
   d. being a president's home

5. **In this article, the word "shipped" means:**
   a. sent only by boat
   b. sent to other places
   c. sent by mail
   d. ships are an important product

6. **Since Ohio has many big cities, we can guess:**
   a. there are no small towns
   b. all of the forests are gone
   c. there are no horses
   d. that many people live in cities

FS-32045 Readin

Name _____

Baseball is often called the national **pastime** because it is so popular in the United States. During the spring and summer months millions of people play this exciting game, while millions of others watch the game and follow the progress of their favorite teams and players.

Baseball began in the eastern United States in the mid 1800's. The National League was founded in 1876 and the American League in 1900.

The game has now **spread** to other parts of the world. It is a major sport in such countries as Canada, Italy, Japan, Taiwan, The Netherlands, South Africa and many Latin American countries. There are organized baseball teams for every age group from 8-year olds to adults.

1. **The best title for this story is:**
   a. Baseball in America
   b. Baseball, An International Sport
   c. The History of Baseball
   d. The Most Popular Sport in the World

2. **Baseball season is mostly:**
   a. the spring months
   b. the fall
   c. the summer months
   d. spring and summer months

3. **Baseball is called a "pastime" because:**
   a. it began in the past
   b. it takes a lot of our most important time
   c. people spend a lot of time watching or playing it
   d. it isn't as important as it was in the past

4. **The article says:**
   a. older people enjoy the sport most
   b. most people just watch
   c. anyone from 8 years of age may join a team
   d. Americans are the best players

5. **The word "spread" as used above means:**
   a. moved to other places
   b. plays baseball
   c. thinks the sport is exciting
   d. put on with a knife

6. **After reading the article we can say the author:**
   a. goes to many games
   b. plays baseball
   c. thinks the sport is exciting
   d. wishes less time were devoted to baseball

California is **probably** the fastest growing state in the Union. Millions of people live here now who did not live here ten years ago.

The Spaniards were the first to explore and settle California. They named Los Angeles and San Francisco.

In 1849, gold was discovered in California and many Americans came to seek riches.

Farmers came to raise crops in the warm climate. Men came to make movies because the sunny weather allowed them to take pictures outdoors nearly every day. Later, oil was discovered and people came to work in the oil fields.

California has many miles of coastline and is therefore a leader in commercial fishing.

1. **The best title for this story is:**
   a. A Beautiful State
   b. Land of the Free
   c. California, Today and Yesterday
   d. The Largest State

2. **The first people who came to settle California were:**
   a. Spaniards
   b. oil workers
   c. movie makers
   d. farmers

3. **The story mentions the farmers just after it tells about:**
   a. the oil workers
   b. the fisherman
   c. the discovery of gold
   d. the movie makers

4. **The word "probably" means:**
   a. most likely
   b. in many cases
   c. definitely
   d. surely

5. **Oilmen, farmers, movie makers and others probably like California most because of the:**
   a. view
   b. many cities
   c. parks and beaches
   d. climate

FS-32045 Reading

Butterflies are the most beautiful of the insects. Poets have called them "winged flowers" and "flying gems." They are found throughout the world.

It is hard to believe that a beautiful butterfly was once a wormlike caterpillar. Caterpillars hatch from the eggs of butterflies and later turn into butterflies. Although the caterpillar eats leaves and fruit and can harm crops, the butterfly does no harm because it can't bite or chew.

Butterflies do not grow in size as they get older. They remain the same size throughout their lifetimes.

No one knows why they are called butterflies. Perhaps it is because many of them are bright yellow like butter.

A good title for this story is:
a. Harmful Caterpillars
b. Catching Butterflies
c. Beautiful Insects
d. The Habits of Butterflies

The story says that butterflies remain the same:
a. size
b. form
c. colors
d. shape

3. **The caterpillar is more harmful to crops than:**
a. the butterfly
b. worms
c. other insects
d. small animals

4. **Butterflies got their name because of:**
a. their color
b. an unknown reason
c. the fact that they looked like butter
d. their softness

5. **In this story, the word "bright" means:**
a. well lit
b. a light or brilliant color
c. smart
d. colorful

6. **Poets gave special names to butterflies because:**
a. they always make up names
b. the names sounded better than butterfly
c. they thought they were as pretty as flowers and jewels
d. the new names were easier to write

81

Soccer **claims** to be the most popular sport in the world. Over one hundred and forty nations belong to its international federation. Other nations also play the game but do not enter international competition.

Every four years the best national soccer teams in the world gather for almost a month to compete for the World Cup.

In 1974, 16 teams competed for the Cup. Defending champion, Brazil, competed against host nation, Germany and 14 other countries. The United States failed to qualify for the World Cup. In the championship game the strong defensive team of West Germany met the strong offensive team from The Netherlands. The West German team was victorious.

1. **The best title for this article is:**
   a. The U.S. Joins Soccer
   b. American Soccer Teams
   c. Soccer, A Major Sport
   d. Learning to Play Soccer

2. **The story says that:**
   a. The U.S. is a major soccer power
   b. The U.S. is not interested
   c. The U.S. tried but did not qualify for the World Cup games
   d. The U.S. will qualify someday

3. **The winner of the World Cup in 1974 was:**
   a. The United States
   b. The Netherlands
   c. West Germany
   d. Russia

4. **The former champion was:**
   a. West Germany
   b. Brazil
   c. The Netherlands
   d. East Germany

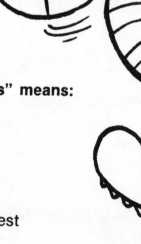

5. **In the article above, the word "claims" means:**
   a. pieces of ground to be farmed
   b. it is so
   c. it is said to be so
   d. an amount of money owed

6. **It is possible to assume that:**
   a. this sport is gaining people's interest
   b. soccer will continue to be popular
   c. other countries will join the competition in the future
   d. all of these are true

FS-32045 Reading

Name _____

A spider is a small, eight-legged animal. Spiders spin webs of silk. They use the webs to catch insects for food.

All spiders spin silk, but some kinds do not make webs. A good example of this is the bolas spider who spins a single line of silk. At the end he spins a **drop** of sticky silk. He swings this line at a nearby insect and traps it in the ball.

All spiders have fangs and most have poison glands. A spider's bite can kill insects and many other small animals, but few spiders are harmful to man. Many people are afraid of spiders, but only hurt or fightened spiders bite man.

Spiders are helpful to man because they eat harmful insects such as locusts which destroy crops, and flies and mosquitos which carry diseases.

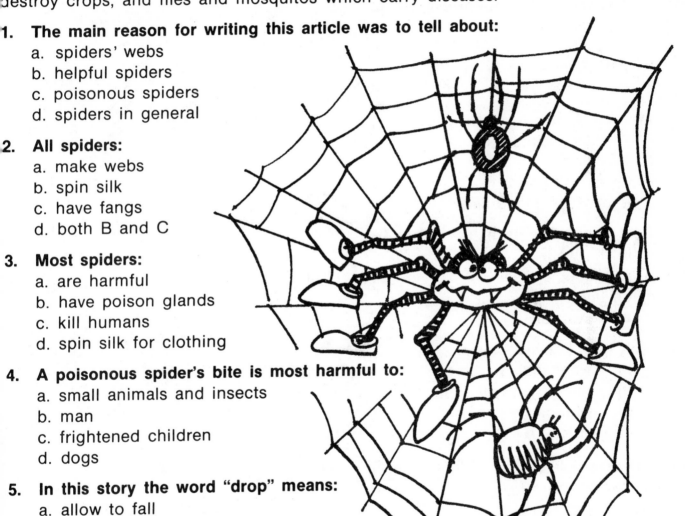

1. **The main reason for writing this article was to tell about:**
   a. spiders' webs
   b. helpful spiders
   c. poisonous spiders
   d. spiders in general

2. **All spiders:**
   a. make webs
   b. spin silk
   c. have fangs
   d. both B and C

3. **Most spiders:**
   a. are harmful
   b. have poison glands
   c. kill humans
   d. spin silk for clothing

4. **A poisonous spider's bite is most harmful to:**
   a. small animals and insects
   b. man
   c. frightened children
   d. dogs

5. **In this story the word "drop" means:**
   a. allow to fall
   b. a small bit of water
   c. a very small amount
   d. a steep cliff with land far below

6. **When you aren't sure a spider is harmless it is best to:**
   a. put it in a jar
   b. call the fire department
   c. leave it alone
   d. pick it up and take it to school to study

83   FS-32045 Reading

A seal is a sleek animal with a body shaped like a bullet. Seals are excellent swimmer and divers. They spend much of their time in the water, but give birth to their youn on land.

Some seals **migrate** about 5,000 miles each year. During the entire trip, the seal swims from 10 to 100 miles from shore, never stopping to touch land. No one know why they make this long yearly trip.

Men hunt seals for their fur and meat which can be used for animal food, poultry food and fertilizer. Seal blubber may be used for cooking or burned for light and heat.

1. **The best title for this article is:**
   a. The Value of Seals
   b. Seals
   c. Why Men Hunt Seals
   d. Where Seals Live

2. **Most seals live in:**
   a. zoos and circuses
   b. fresh water
   c. lakes and ponds
   d. oceans or inland seas

3. **Seal babies are born:**
   a. in the water
   b. in a special nest
   c. on land
   d. in the ocean

4. **Men hunt seals because:**
   a. they want their fur
   b. they want the meat
   c. their blubber is useful
   d. all of these reasons

5. **The word "migrate" means:**
   a. swim
   b. travel
   c. eat
   d. have babies

6. **Although man doesn't really understand why seals migrate, the seal probably:**
   a. does it because he likes to swim long distances
   b. likes the foods in other places
   c. likes a vacation
   d. has a reason known only to other seals

FS-32045 Reading

On the surface a submarine operates much like any other ship. It has a rudder and stern and can be handled like other surface ships.

In order to dive, the submarine takes water into its ballast tanks by releasing air pressure that kept the water out.

When it is submerged, it **switches** to battery-driven electric motors. Nuclear-powered submarines continue to use their normal engines. By adjusting its diving planes, the sub can move up and down in the water.

In order to rise to the surface the submarine sets its diving planes to rise and blows all the water from its ballast tanks.

The best title for this article is:
a. How Submarines Submerge
b. How Submarines Operate
c. How Subs Rise
d. Parts of a Submarine

Submarines may be handled much like other ships when:
a. they are submerged
b. they are on the surface
c. they are nuclear powered
d. the ballast tanks are full

3. **Submarines dive by:**
a. letting out the air pressure
b. filling the tanks with fish
c. emptying the ballast tanks
d. putting up the periscope

4. **The diving planes are used to help the sub:**
a. move up and down in the water
b. to fly
c. to help the sub rise
d. both A and C

5. **In this story, the word "switches" means:**
a. buttons to push
b. changes
c. things that can cause a machine to work
d. connections to lights

6. **Probably the parts of a submarine that make it most unlike other ships are the:**
a. rudders
b. the ballast tanks
c. the sterns
d. the nuclear power

FS-32045 Reading

Read each paragraph. Decide which answer tells the main idea and circle it.

1. Somebody is moving in under my front porch today. Only it's not a somebody. It's a somebuggy. A whole lot of somebuggies, to be exact! I watched quietly from the top of the stairs. A family of 300 ants came marching along. First in line were the baby ants. They looked very tired.

    a. a moving porch   b. somebuggies moving day   c. the somebuggy march

2. The biggest ant led the way. I called him Chief. He directed all the traffic. It was a good thing Chief had six legs. He could point six different ways at once. Here. There. Left. Right. Straight ahead. In no time, Chief had all the baby ants moved into their rooms.

    a. how many legs ants have
    b. directing ant traffic
    c. what a Chief does

3. Next came the worker ants. They carried all the food. Tiny pieces of cupcake, bread, potato chips and one olive passed right by my nose. Well, well! I'll bet someone in the park is missing his picnic lunch. The last ant had a tiny box on his back. It was a Bingo game.

    a. a picnic lunch   b. games worker ants play   c. what worker ants carry

4. Last in line was the Queen. Fifteen ants held an umbrella over her. Ants get hot, too, I guess. At last, the ants were all moved in. I hope they don't make a lot of noise. It's fun having somebuggy under my porch. Maybe some more somebuggies will move in tomorrow.

    a. my new neighbors
    b. why ants get hot
    c. coming of the Queen

─── **Thinking Time** ───

Read the next two questions carefully. Answer them on the back of this paper.

1. Ants often have to move to new homes or "nests". Why do they probably have to move?

2. Ants are insects. They have six legs. Name other insects that you know about or have caught.

FS-32045 Readin

Name _____ **Date** _____

Read each paragraph. Decide which answer best tells the <u>main idea</u> and circle it.

1. Most animals have tails. But many other things have tails, too. Kites have tails made of string. An airplane's tail helps it to fly. The bottom of your shirt has a tail, but it doesn't help you fly. Lots of little girls wear pigtails—but they don't look anything like a pig's tail.

    a. funny names for tails   b. different kinds of tails   c. why we have tails

2. Did you know your eyebrows can talk? Lifted way up, they say "Surprise!" Down, way down, says you're mad. Move them together so they meet across your nose. That means you are worried. Next time you look in a mirror, make a face. Did your eyebrows say anything?

    a. how eyebrows talk
    b. how to make eyebrows move
    c. watching your eyebrows

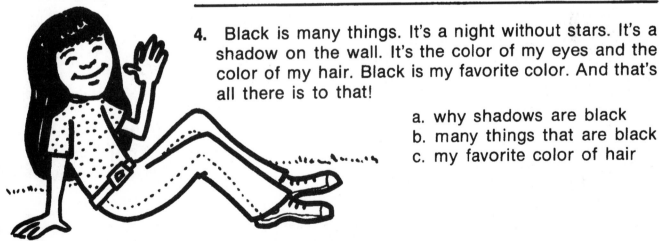

3. Have you ever seen a whirligig? It's a strange insect that lives in ponds. It spins around in water like a mad bee. Whirligigs have funny eyes. Each eye has two halves. One half looks up. The other half looks down—at the same time. Don't try to catch a whirligig. They smell awful.

    a. an unusual insect   b. strange-looking eyes   c. how whirligigs smell

4. Black is many things. It's a night without stars. It's a shadow on the wall. It's the color of my eyes and the color of my hair. Black is my favorite color. And that's all there is to that!

    a. why shadows are black
    b. many things that are black
    c. my favorite color of hair

——————————— **Thinking Time** ———————————

Read the next two questions carefully. Answer them on the back of this paper.

1. There are many different kinds of bags. How many different kinds of bags can you think of?

2. What is your favorite color? Think of three things of that color that are unusual.

Name _____ Date _____

Read each paragraph. Decide which answer best tells the main idea and circle it.

1. Have you ever heard someone say: "He's wise as an owl?" Owls may look wise but they really aren't. Now take the elephant. That's a smart animal. He learns very quickly. You always see elephant acts at the circus. But have you ever seen owl acts?

   a. a smart bird   b. a funny saying   c. a circus act

2. With your fingerprints, you can make all different kinds of faces. Dot a few dots, draw some lines and your prints can say many things: happy, sad, angry, afraid, worried. A fingerprint can even become a ladybug or a turtle. Make some fingerprints of your own. Draw in pictures of other animals.

   a. how many fingers you have
   b. how to draw a face
   c. things to make from fingerprints

3. If you see a red spider, make a wish, quick! Then jump around in a circle on one foot. Make a sound just like a bee flying backwards. And just to make sure, count to 25 three times. Now, if you can still remember what you wished for, it will come true tomorrow.

   a. the red spider wish   b. how to make wishes   c. how to fly backwards

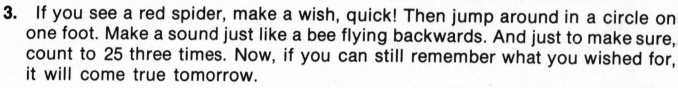

4. Why is a butterfly called a butterfly? He can fly, that's for sure. But he's not made of butter. Are there only "lady" ladybugs? Nope. There are as many male-ladybugs as lady-ladybugs. There must be better names for butterflies and ladybugs.

   a. insects with funny names
   b. insects made of butter
   c. giving an insect a new name

──────── **Thinking Time** ────────

Read the next two questions carefully. Answer them on the back of this paper.

1. If you wanted something very much, what would you do to make your wish come true?

2. A rabbicoon is part rabbit and part raccoon. From the names of the next four animals, make up two silly names and get two new animals: kangaroo, moose, turtle, seal.

88

FS-32045 Readin

Name _____ **Date** _____

Read each paragraph. Decide which answer best tells the <u>main idea</u> and circle it.

1. I started out as a seed, but a very special seed, as you will see. One day (before I was a bud) little leaves sprang up out of the earth. Yup! It was Spring. Time for leaves to grow.

   a. beginning of Spring   b. a warm day   c. when the earth starts to grow

2. Pretty soon, it was my turn to make an appearance. At first, I was a little bud on a big leaf. All day, I just sat around in the sun. What a life! I got bigger, fatter and rounder. I looked terrific!

   a. sitting in the sun all day
   b. a big, fat leaf
   c. life as a leaf

3. Farmer Mike walked through the fields. He stopped right near my vine. "What happened here?" he asked, scratching his head. "A purple pumpkin in my patch! I'm afraid no one will want that one for Halloween."

   a. Farmer Mike's patch   b. a Halloween pumpkin   c. a strange pumpkin

4. Oh sob! Halloween night all alone. I'm a failure as a pumpkin. Later on, Missy Tissy came to the patch. She tripped over my stem and screamed: A GIANT GRAPE. The whole world will want to see this! I felt so happy. I really wasn't a pumpkin after all.

   a. all alone on Halloween
   b. a happy ending
   c. a screaming grape

───── **Thinking Time** ─────

Read the next two questions carefully. Answer them on the back of this paper.

1. Pumpkins are big, round, orange and grow on a vine. Describe everything you can about a banana.

2. In Spring everything starts to bloom and grow. What begins to happen to plants, trees and flowers in the Fall?

Read each paragraph. Decide which answer best tells the <u>main idea</u> and circle it.

1. Yesterday I passed by Connie's Candy Corner. They are having a contest. "Win a Whizzer Bike," the sign read. "Just guess the number of jelly beans in this jar. Bring in your guess and drop it in the box before 3 o'clock on Thursday."

   a. a Win-A-Bike contest   b. guessing jelly beans   c. winning a contest

2. How am I going to win that contest? Hm-m-m-m. I've got it! I'll buy a jar just like the one in the candy store. Then I'll buy some jelly beans. One by one I'll drop them into the jar until it is full. My little sister can write down the numbers. Her reward for helping me will be fifteen red jelly beans.

   a. planning a contest
   b. a plan to win
   c. a way to count

3. At last, the day arrived. Everyone crowded into the candy store at 4 o'clock. "We have a tie," Connie announced. "Fourteen people guessed the same number! I wonder how that happened? We'll just have to have a tie-breaker." Everyone who was correct, get ready!

   a. how to break ties   b. fourteen guesses   c. a winning tie

4. Connie lifted out another jar. It was filled with peanuts. "Everyone gets one guess—right now!" My guess didn't win—I was off by 600 peanuts. Oh, well. At least I have 1304 jelly beans to eat when I get home.

   a. how I lost the contest
   b. the number of peanuts
   c. a winner by 600 peanuts

―――――――― **Thinking Time** ――――――――

Read the next two questions carefully. Answer them on the back of this paper.

1. I lost the contest, but that's OK. I'll enter another contest tomorrow. I like contests. What is the main idea of this story?

2. Read #4. Why did Connie have everyone guess the number of peanuts right then?

Read each paragraph. Decide which answer best tells the <u>main idea</u> and circle it.

1. An elephant is very lucky. He carries his shower around with him. If an elephant gets dirty, he can just turn on his trunk. There is one funny thing about elephants, though. First, they get themselves all clean. Then they go sit in the mud. I wish I could do that, too.

   a. how elephants clean their trunks
   b. when elephants take showers
   c. some funny things about elephants

2. Have you ever seen: An ox in a box? A clam eating ham? A duck saying "cluck"? A fly wearing a tie? A moose flying on a goose? A seal shopping for a meal? Or a bear with blonde curly hair?

   a. some strange animals b. animals I've seen c. new animals to see

3. Click! Your pen is ready to write. Long ago, getting ready to write was not so easy. Everyone had to make their own pens, called quills. Quill pens were made from feathers. Turkey feathers were used most often. But a swan feather made the best pen.

   a. the best kind of pen
   b. pens used long ago
   c. feathers made from pens

4. I'm making a cake for my sister's birthday. Am I nice! Now watch carefully. You might want to make my Oozie Doozie Cake someday. Start with 2 cups mint chip ice cream. Add 4 grapes, 1 cup smashed peas, 25 eggs, chopped lettuce and some peanut butter. That's it.

   a. making green ice cream b. an Oozie Doozie boy c. making a birthday cake

———— Thinking Time ————

Read the next two questions carefully. Answer them on the back of this paper.

1. Use the next five animal names and make them do something strange, like the animals in story # 2: Cat, frog, cow, ant, bunny.

2. If you could make your favorite cake, what five things would it have in it?

Name _____ **Date** _____

Read each paragraph. Decide which answer best tells the <u>main idea</u> and circle it.

1. Does anyone want a little sister? I've got one I'd like to give away. Yesterday, my Mom had to go shopping. "I'll be back at one o'clock. You take good care of Patty," she said. I asked Patty what she wanted to do. That was my first mistake.

    a. giving sisters away
    b. sitting on my sister
    c. babysitting a little sister

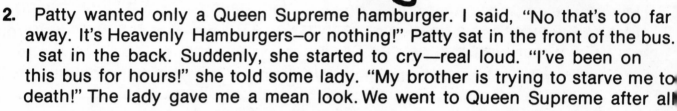

2. Patty wanted only a Queen Supreme hamburger. I said, "No that's too far away. It's Heavenly Hamburgers—or nothing!" Patty sat in the front of the bus. I sat in the back. Suddenly, she started to cry—real loud. "I've been on this bus for hours!" she told some lady. "My brother is trying to starve me to death!" The lady gave me a mean look. We went to Queen Supreme after all.

    a. eating on the bus   b. Patty gets her way   c. Patty's favorite hamburger

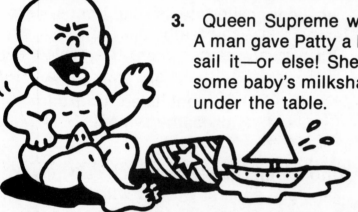

3. Queen Supreme was very crowded. We had to wait. A man gave Patty a Burger Boat to make. I told her not to sail it—or else! She did it anyway. It landed right in some baby's milkshake. The baby screamed. I crawled under the table.

    a. getting into trouble
    b. making babies scream
    c. the trouble with Burger Boats

4. Back home, Patty brought her Bing-Bang game into the living room—and tripped. How was I going to clean up 3,000 marbles? Just then Mom came home. "Look what he did!" Patty cried. I went to my room and locked the door. In three days, I might come out again, but not before.

    a. making sisters happy   b. a long rest   c. a crazy day

─────────────────── **Thinking Time** ───────────────────

Read the next two questions carefully. Answer them on the back of this paper.

1. Pretend you are baby-sitting for Patty. Name 3 things you would do to keep her out of trouble.

2. Patty said her brother ruined her game. What do you think their mother said?

92   FS-32045 Readir

Name _____ **Date** _____

Read each paragraph. Decide which answer best tells the <u>main idea</u> and circle it.

1. "Well here we are," said City Rat. "It's nice to be at the beach for a change." City Rat banged on a bell. "A room, please—for 80," he told Beach Rat. "Nice hotel you have here. How's the garbage? Good? Well, that's fine. We'll take a table in the alley at 8 o'clock. See you then."

a. moving to the beach
b. where rats live
c. rats on a vacation

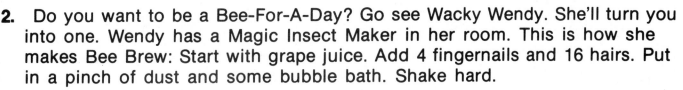

2. Do you want to be a Bee-For-A-Day? Go see Wacky Wendy. She'll turn you into one. Wendy has a Magic Insect Maker in her room. This is how she makes Bee Brew: Start with grape juice. Add 4 fingernails and 16 hairs. Put in a pinch of dust and some bubble bath. Shake hard.

a. how insects are brewed   b. a magic Bee Brew   c. a grape and dust drink

3. One day, I saw a mouse near the P Z B & M Market. He looked so lonely. I invited him to come home with me. That night he went to sleep by my window. Next morning: "What is this!" my mother screamed. "Your mouse has invited his whole family over here! I guess I should be glad you didn't find a lonely elephant and bring him home!"

a. a mouse that found an elephant
b. a lonely mouse finds a home
c. scaring my mother

4. "I'm sorry, Arthur. Doug can't come out and play," his father said. "Late last night, it finally happened. Doug turned into a TV. We called the doctor. He couldn't do a thing for Doug. I guess we'll have to wait until he blows a tube. Then maybe he'll turn back into Doug again."

a. blowing a tube   b. what happened to Doug   c. getting sick from TV

—————— **Thinking Time** ——————

Read the next two questions carefully. Answer them on the back of this paper.

1. If you were only five inches tall, what would you be? What could you do that you can't do now?

2. Why did Doug turn into a TV? Draw a picture of what he probably looked like.

Name _____ Date _____

Read each paragraph. Decide which answer best tells the main idea and circle it.

1. I heard my dog Wolfgang barking. He was down in the
basement. There's a ghost living down there, you know.
I wondered if he caught my dog. Wolfgang barked
louder and louder. He sounded frightened. I thought, "I
must save him!"

   a. a frightened dog
   b. a lost boy
   c. a barking ghost

2. Slowly, I opened the basement door. I had my mother's mop, just in case.
Wolfgang stopped barking, but I couldn't see him anywhere. It was mostly dark,
only a little sunlight. Something moved! It was near the washing machine.
WHAM! I hit a pile of clothes. WHAM, again. "Where's my dog!" I yelled.

   a. hunting for a dog   b. mopping up clothes   c. hitting piles of clothes

3. Clothes were everywhere! I spilled some soap, too.
But no ghost. Did I miss him? Next I crept over to an
open window. I had my mop all ready to clobber
the ghost. Suddenly, something licked my nose. It was
Wolfgang! He had escaped from the ghost.

   a. the clothes escape
   b. escaping out of windows
   c. the return of Wolfgang

4. A minute later, my Mom turned on the light. She was not very happy. Her
clean wash was all over the floor. I explained to her about the terrible ghost.
"But I got him! I hit him with this mop. WHAM. He'll never come back here again.
I saved Wolfgang's life. Aren't you proud of me?"

   a. how to scare a ghost   b. a very brave boy   c. a very mad mother

———————————————— **Thinking Time** ————————————————

Read the next two questions. Answer them on the back of this paper.

1. <u>Clothes</u> were everywhere! What other way can you spell the underlined word?
Use it in a sentence.

2. When somebody is said to be "white as a ghost" how do you think that person
looks and feels?

94

FS-32045 Reading

ead each paragraph. Decide which answer best tells the <u>main idea</u> and circle it.

Here's a trick to try on one of your friends. Have her stand against a wall. The right side of her shoe and her shoulder are against the wall. Now ask her to lift her left leg off the floor. Could she do it?

a. playing a trick on a friend
b. the best place for doing tricks
c. trying out tricks on a wall

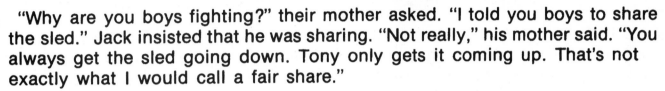

"Why are you boys fighting?" their mother asked. "I told you boys to share the sled." Jack insisted that he was sharing. "Not really," his mother said. "You always get the sled going down. Tony only gets it coming up. That's not exactly what I would call a fair share."

a. learning to share   b. an unfair share   c. a sled for two

3. Finish this rhyme:

Three tall men were sitting in a tree.
An owl came along and sat on one knee.
"Don't stay here, this is not your nest,

_____

a. making up the end of a rhyme
b. finding a word to rhyme with nest
c. finishing a story about trees

"Thanksgiving Day comes inn November. My fomily meats for dinner at 4 o'clock. Last year, my Dad red a special story. I wish he wood do it again this year." Some words in the story are not spelled correctly. Can you find them? Cross them out. Write the correct spelling above the word.

a. two ways to spell   b. finding misspelled words   c. a spell-binding story

────────────── **Thinking Time** ──────────────

Read the next two questions carefully. Answer them on the back of this paper.

1. Some tricks are dangerous. People can get hurt. You should not hit or trip anyone. The trick isn't funny anymore. Write the main idea.

. 'Fair' and 'fare' sound the same, but have different meanings. Use each one in a sentence.

Read each paragraph. Decide which answer best tells the main idea and circle it.

1. My dad has a rule: No one leaves the dinner table until everyone finishes eating. You might think that's a good rule. But you don't know my little brother. His name is Jeff. I think Jeff is half-snail. He is very slow.

   a. eating at a table
   b. a dinner time rule
   c. little boys who eat snails

2. Last night we had peas for dinner. Jeff ate all his peas—one-by-one! Then we had hot cheese sandwiches. Jeff took 50 teeny tiny bites, then held up the sandwich. He chewed a capital T into the toast. One hour and Jeff still hadn't finished eating!

   a. peas and cheese for dinner   b. how to make a T   c. a very long dinner hour

3. Jeff is driving me crazy! I have to find a way to make him eat faster. Tonight, my favorite show, Long Lost Larry, is on TV. I'm working on a speedy-eating plan right now.

   a. a plan for Jeff   b. a favorite TV show   c. a boy goes crazy

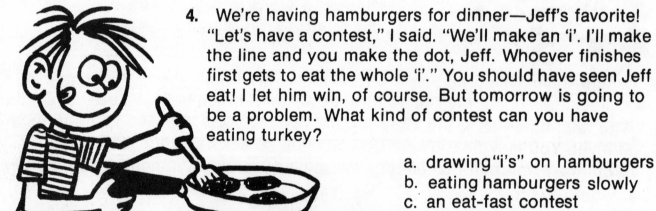

4. We're having hamburgers for dinner—Jeff's favorite! "Let's have a contest," I said. "We'll make an 'i'. I'll make the line and you make the dot, Jeff. Whoever finishes first gets to eat the whole 'i'." You should have seen Jeff eat! I let him win, of course. But tomorrow is going to be a problem. What kind of contest can you have eating turkey?

   a. drawing "i's" on hamburgers
   b. eating hamburgers slowly
   c. an eat-fast contest

―――――――― **Thinking Time** ――――――――

Read the next two questions carefully. Answer them on the back of this paper.

1. Make up a long sentence using all four of these words: goat, trumpet, gum, skating.

2. "Jeff eats slowly. He swallows much too fast. It takes him hours to eat." One sentence doesn't fit. Cross it out and write another one that fits the story better.

Read each paragraph. Decide which answer tells the main idea and circle it.

. Have you ever had a piece of shoo-fly pie? No, it is not made of flies. This pie got its name long, long ago. After baking, a pie was set by a window to cool. Flies could smell the pie miles away. Hundreds would zoom over. Somebody had to stand by the window and shoo the flies away all day.

a. how shoo-fly pie got its name
b. a good name for pies with flies
c. why flies like shoo-fly pie

2. "Boy, I slept like a baby last night." That means that you probably slept for ten hours. Now you feel all rested. But, if you want to feel really, really rested—sleep like a gorilla! Gorillas sleep for fourteen hours at a stretch. They never even have time to get tired.

a. how long babies sleep   b. how to sleep soundly   c. how to feel rested

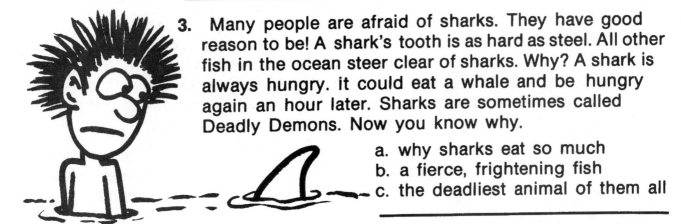

3. Many people are afraid of sharks. They have good reason to be! A shark's tooth is as hard as steel. All other fish in the ocean steer clear of sharks. Why? A shark is always hungry. it could eat a whale and be hungry again an hour later. Sharks are sometimes called Deadly Demons. Now you know why.

a. why sharks eat so much
b. a fierce, frightening fish
c. the deadliest animal of them all

4. The next time you sneeze, try not to close your eyes. No one has been able to do it yet. You may be the first. Do you know how fast that sneeze travels? About 100 miles per hour! You never knew your nose had so much power, did you?

a. where a sneeze travels   b. facts about sneezes   c. facts about noses

————————— **Thinking Time** —————————

Read the next two questions carefully. Answer them on the back of this paper.

1. There is a cookie called a "snickerdoodle". Make up a story about how the cookie got its name.

2. "Sleep like a baby" means you sleep a long time. What does "sleep like a log" mean?

Name _____ Date _____

Read each paragraph. Decide which answer best tells the main idea and circle it.

1. I'm going to tell you three things. Then you tell me who might say them: "How do you feel? Stick out your tongue. Say Ah-h-h." If you guessed a doctor, you're right. Word clues can help you name many different people. You know who they are by the special words they use. What would be some good clues for a teacher?

   a. finding the right words
   b. how to name a doctor
   c. a word clue game

2. There are many ways to discover new things. Experiments are a fun way to discover. Some experiments you can do easily at home. Others your teacher can help you do. Discovering things for yourself is exciting! All you have to do is watch, listen and try.

   a. experimenting at home b. ways to discover c. ways to do experiments

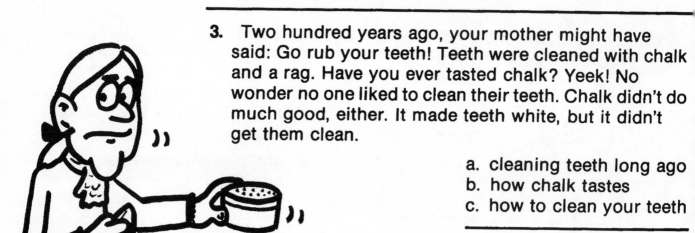

3. Two hundred years ago, your mother might have said: Go rub your teeth! Teeth were cleaned with chalk and a rag. Have you ever tasted chalk? Yeek! No wonder no one liked to clean their teeth. Chalk didn't do much good, either. It made teeth white, but it didn't get them clean.

   a. cleaning teeth long ago
   b. how chalk tastes
   c. how to clean your teeth

4. There was an old woman who lived in a tent,
   She had three dollars and 40 cents.
   "I need some carrots for my Foo-Fum stew.
   This money should buy me four thousand and two."

a. how much carrots cost b. an old woman's wish c. where an old woman lives

───────────── **Thinking Time** ─────────────

Read the next two questions. Answer them on the back of this paper.

1. Why would a toothbrush be much better than a rag for cleaning your teeth?

2. "A dinosaur once stood on my toe." Write the next line. The last word should rhyme with "toe".

                FS-32045 Reading

Name _____ Date _____

Read each paragraph. Decide which answer best tells the <u>main idea</u> and circle it.

1. How would you like to have a flea circus? First of all, catch a bunch of fleas. Then make a little stage for the flea act. Fleas really can do tricks. They'll jump through hoops. They'll even pull a tiny paper wagon around!

   a. how fleas jump through hoops
   b. going to a flea circus
   c. putting on a flea circus

2. Do you see flashing lights over there? Those are fireflies. They really light up a dark sky. Try to catch some in a jar. Their light is so bright you could read this page by them.

   a. firefly facts   b. reading by firefly light   c. catching fireflies

3. There are hundreds of different kinds of ice cream. Rooty-Tooty is my favorite. This ice cream tastes good with everything: bananas, peas, hamburgers, toast and tomatoes, too. Tonight I'm having Rooty-Tooty Turkey. I warm up some Rooty-Tooty in a pan and pour it over the turkey. Best gravy in the whole world!

   a. ice cream that tastes like gravy
   b. how Rooty-Tooty Turkey tastes
   c. go-with-everything ice cream

slurp

4. The football game is over. Your friends are leaving the field. You want to know if your team won. There are two ways you could find out: Ask someone. Or, better, look at everyone's face. Do they look sad and unhappy? Now you can probably guess who won. Faces can tell all different feelings and moods without anyone saying a word.

   a. a winning team   b. finding out who won   c. what faces can tell you

──────────────── **Thinking Time** ────────────────

Read the next two questions. Answer them on the back of this page.

1. You are going to make an ice cream sundae. It is called Heaven-Help-Us. Name all the things you are going to put on your sundae.

2. John's bike was ruined. His brother left it out in the rain. Write a sentence or draw a picture to describe John's face.

Name _____ **Date** _____

Read each paragraph. Decide which answer best tells the <u>main idea</u> and circle it.

1. There are many different things you can do with gum. Some of them are bad. Let's think of a few fun things first. You can chew it. You can blow bubbles. You could even fix a broken model airplane with some chewed gum (just in case you run out of glue).

   a. how gum is different
   b. the many uses of gum
   c. why gum is good

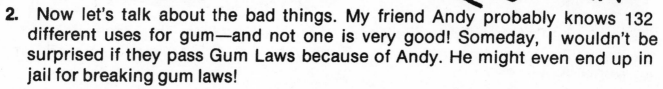

2. Now let's talk about the bad things. My friend Andy probably knows 132 different uses for gum—and not one is very good! Someday, I wouldn't be surprised if they pass Gum Laws because of Andy. He might even end up in jail for breaking gum laws!

   a. passing a Gum Law   b. 132 uses for gum   c. about Andy and gum

3. On wash day, Andy's mother found a pack of gum in his shirt pocket. But only after she pulled it out of the dryer! All the clothes were ruined! At night, Andy sticks his old gum under his bed. One day, the cat went to sleep under there. They had to call a vet to come over and cut off all the cat's fur. The cat had to wear a sweater after that.

   a. bad uses for gum
   b. where cats take a nap
   c. ruining clothes in the dryer

4. "That's it! The gum goes or you go!" Andy's mother stated. But Andy had an idea. He would make a Used Gum Holder. Every day he puts a piece of tape over his belt. This is how it works: Pull up piece of tape. Stick gum to belt. Smooth tape over again. At the end of day, tape will pull gum off belt. And that's the end of Andy's story.

   a. a good idea for gum   b. taping gum to belts   c. a very angry mother

———————————— **Thinking Time** ————————————

Read the next two questions carefully. Answer them on the back of this paper.

1. Andy would like to stop chewing gum. What could you invent for him to help him stop chewing? Draw a picture of it.

2. If some Gum Laws were really passed, name four DON'Ts that would be on the list for sure.

100   FS-32045 Readin

Name _____ Date _____

Read each paragraph. Decide which answer best tells the main idea and circle it.

1. While searching for my lost bike, my head brushed against a foot. It belonged to the giant, Jasper. He was fast asleep high in a tree. Jasper sleeps all summer long. Hot weather makes him very grouchy!

   a. sleeping through the summer   b. a sleeping giant   c. long summer days

---

2. Carefully, I climbed up the tree. One of Jasper's coat pockets clanged and banged in the wind. When the wind stopped, I jumped into his pocket. You won't believe what's in here! Has Jasper moved all his furniture out of his cave?

   a. climbing into a giant's pocket
   b. pockets full of wind
   c. a surprise in a pocket

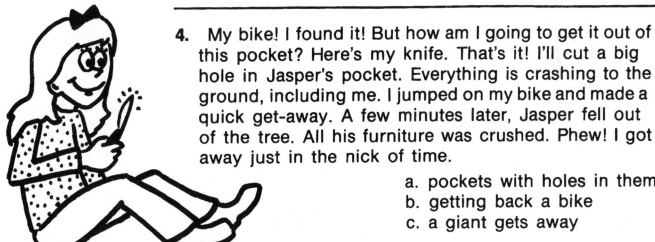

3. Deep inside the pocket, Jasper's grandfather clock is still ticking. A bathtub, over to the left a little, has a set of encyclopedias stacked inside. Jasper's refrigerator and TV are here, too. What is this behind the sofa? Well! What do you know!

   a. furniture made for pockets   b. hiding behind sofas   c. a giant's furniture

---

4. My bike! I found it! But how am I going to get it out of this pocket? Here's my knife. That's it! I'll cut a big hole in Jasper's pocket. Everything is crashing to the ground, including me. I jumped on my bike and made a quick get-away. A few minutes later, Jasper fell out of the tree. All his furniture was crushed. Phew! I got away just in the nick of time.

   a. pockets with holes in them
   b. getting back a bike
   c. a giant gets away

──────────── **Thinking Time** ────────────

Read the next two questions carefully. Answer them on the back of this paper.

1. Hot weather makes Jasper grouchy and mean. Name three things that make you feel grouchy.

2. A hole is an opening. What is another way to spell the word 'hole'? Write the meaning.

Name _____ **Date** _____

Read each paragraph. Decide which answer best tells the <u>main idea</u> and circle it.

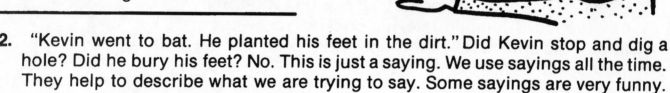

1. Guess what I am? I turn around, but I don't go anywhere. I'm fastened to a door and locked with a key. Sometimes I'm polished, sometimes I'm painted. Muddy hands and fingerprints are all over me.

    a. how to describe a lock
    b. how a doorknob is described
    c. how to figure out riddles

2. "Kevin went to bat. He planted his feet in the dirt." Did Kevin stop and dig a hole? Did he bury his feet? No. This is just a saying. We use sayings all the time. They help to describe what we are trying to say. Some sayings are very funny.

    a. why we use sayings   b. sayings about plants   c. how to plant feet

3. Poems about yourself are the best poems of all. Read this one. Then write another poem using your own name.

    B orn in Scott, Kentucky
    E nd of May is his birthday
    N ine years old

    a. short names
    b. poems about yourself
    c. words that rhyme with me

4. Joanie sent a message to her friends. They all belong to the Scutter Secret Club. This is what the note said: I don't feel 2 good. It must be something I 8. What was it—the black-I'd P's or Mom's 5-layer cake? I'll go C a doctor. He'll know what 2 do 4 me.

    a. how Joanie got sick   b. a person who can't spell   c. writing a secret code

―――――――――――――――Thinking Time―――――――――――――――

Read the next two questions. Answer them on the back of this paper.

1. Make up some clues to describe a flag. Read them to a friend one-by-one. How many clues did you have to give before he guessed it?

2. Write your name or nickname down the side of a page just like #3. Now write a short poem telling something about yourself.

102   FS-32045 Reading

Name _____ Date _____

Read each paragraph. Decide which answer best tells the main idea and circle it.

1. Norway is sometimes called the Land of the Midnight Sun. The sun shining at midnight? That's right. During June and July, the sun never sets. It is daytime all the time. But this happens for only two months. Just think how much electricity is saved.

   a. who lives in the Land of the Midnight Sun
   b. a place where it is daytime year round
   c. a place where the sun shines at midnight

2. Do you have a pesty little sister? I do. She used to come in my room a lot. But I fixed that! Do you want to know how to do it, too? Keep all kinds of squishy things in your room: snails, worms, dead plants and a few snakes. My little sister doesn't even come near me any more!(Neither does anyone else!)

   a. keeping sisters out   b. fixing your room   c. sisters that are pests

3. Yesterday, I whacked my funny bone on a door. It wasn't the least bit funny! I could feel the pain all the way to my toes. This bone needs another name.

   a. a bone that is not fun
   b. a funny name for a bone
   c. a bone that hurts the toes

4. I had to write a story. The title was: Who Would You Like to Invite to Dinner? And this is what I wrote: I would like to ask a brontosaurus to dinner—every night. He loves vegetables and I don't. Our apartment is on the fifth floor. A brontosaurus is five stories tall, too. His mouth would fit perfectly at the kitchen window. That's who I would like to invite to dinner.

   a. a story about dinner   b. the best guest   c. dinner on the fifth floor

───────────────── **Thinking Time** ─────────────────

Read the next two questions carefully. Answer them on the back of this paper.

1. Why would it be difficult to live where the sun shines all day and all night?
2. Hurt means _____ . The opposite of this word is _____ .
   How has someone hurt your feelings?

Name _____ Date _____

Read each paragraph. Decide which answer best tells the __main idea__ and circle it

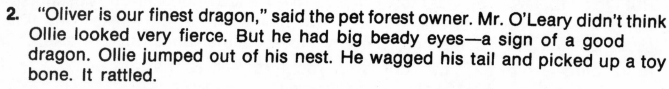

1. Long, long ago, there was a family named O'Leary.
They lived in a castle. One summer, the O'Learys
wanted to go on vacation. "Our castle
doesn't have any locks," Mr. O'Leary said.
"We need to get a good
dragon to guard our gold."

   a. planning a summer vacation
   b. looking for a castle guard
   c. where the O'Leary family lived

2. "Oliver is our finest dragon," said the pet forest owner. Mr. O'Leary didn't think
Ollie looked very fierce. But he had big beady eyes—a sign of a good
dragon. Ollie jumped out of his nest. He wagged his tail and picked up a toy
bone. It rattled.

   a. picking out a dragon b. a friendly pet c. leaving the nest

3. "Good-bye, Ollie," waved the O'Learys. "Take good
care of our castle and our gold." Early Sunday,
three men sneaked up on the bridge. Ollie sat up on his
tail. He tried to roar. It sounded like "yip-yip." He
tried to breathe fire. Only a little steam poured out.
Ollie cried.

   a. a very soft roar
   b. leaving for vacation
   c. trying to guard a castle

4. "Look, it's only a baby dragon!" The men felt sorry for Ollie. "Let's make him
a hero." Inside the castle, the men tossed around some furniture. "Stand
here in front of the gold, Ollie. The O'Learys will be home soon. They will think
you scared us away." Ollie was so happy. Tomorrow he would practice his
roar and his fire.

   a. a happy ending b. ruining a castle c. a little dragon comes home

———————————————— Thinking Time ————————————————

Read the next two questions. Answer them on the back of this paper.

1. In story #1, find a word that means "to take a trip." Now write two things about
the last trip you took (even if it was just to the store).

2. Read story #2. How could you tell Ollie was just a baby dragon?

            FS-32045 Reading

Answer Key

Name _____

A Bear Who's Not a Bear

Everyone knows what a teddy bear looks like. A **koala** bear, who's really not a bear, looks a lot like your favorite teddy. When a koala is born he is only about an inch long. <u>He</u> crawls into his mother's pocket for six months. For three months longer he hangs on her back. This fuzzy, bushy-tailed animal eats only one kind of food. All night long he munches the leaves of the blue gum tree. During the day he sleeps in its branches. In the past the koala were hunted for their beautiful gray and white fur. Today the **Australian** government protects them.

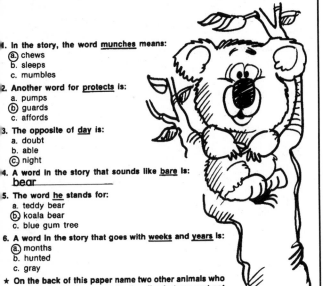

1. In the story, the word <u>munches</u> means:
   a. chews ✓
   b. sleeps
   c. mumbles
2. Another word for <u>protects</u> is:
   a. pumps
   b. guards ✓
   c. affords
3. The opposite of <u>day</u> is:
   a. doubt
   b. able
   c. night ✓
4. A word in the story that sounds like <u>bare</u> is:
   bear
5. The word <u>he</u> stands for:
   a. teddy bear
   b. koala bear ✓
   c. blue gum tree
6. A word in the story that goes with <u>weeks</u> and <u>years</u> is:
   a. months ✓
   b. hunted
   c. gray

★ On the back of this paper name two other animals who live in trees. Write about why they live in trees and not on the ground.

Page 1

Name _____

The American Bird

High on a cliff, bald eagle eggs are warmed by both parents. Both feed the newly hatched **eaglets** and guard the nest. The eaglets' soft down turns to gray or brown feathers at age two. At four, the head, neck and tail become white. The bill, feet and part of the toes turn to bright yellow. In the early morning, eagles hunt for small animals, snakes and birds. <u>They</u> eat, rest and fly. They soar faster than 100 miles per hour. The bald eagle is the bird that stands for the United States. You can see his picture on a dollar bill.

1. In the story, the word <u>high</u> means:
   a. far above the ground ✓
   b. on the ground
   c. below the ground
2. Another word for <u>hunt</u> is:
   a. lose
   b. allow
   c. seek ✓
3. The opposite of <u>bright</u> is:
   a. bring
   b. dull ✓
   c. safe
4. A word in the story that sounds like <u>sore</u> is:
   soar
5. The word <u>they</u> stands for:
   a. eagles ✓
   b. snakes
   c. dollar bills
6. A word in the story that goes with <u>noon</u> and <u>evening</u> is:
   a. faster
   b. picture
   c. morning ✓

★ The bald eagle is dying out. On the back of this paper, write what you can do to protect the eagle.

Page 2

Name _____

It's Freezing Here

The **Antarctic** Ocean is a cold place to live. Yet, <u>it</u> is home to thousands of whales and millions of seals. **Penguins** live here too. They swim with their wings to find fish for supper. Then they sun themselves on ice islands. The largest animal that ever lived in this ocean is the blue whale. This animal can grow to be longer than thirteen automobiles placed end to end. Most of the water in this ocean freezes during the winter. In October, the solid ice packs break into huge chunks.

1. In the story, the word <u>ocean</u> means:
   a. a small body of water
   b. a lake
   c. a large body of water ✓
2. Another word for <u>home</u> is:
   a. house ✓
   b. car
   c. pony
3. The opposite of <u>cold</u> is:
   a. freezing
   b. cool
   c. hot ✓
4. A word in the story that sounds like <u>blew</u> is:
   blue
5. The word <u>It</u> stands for:
   a. the blue whale
   b. the Antarctic Ocean ✓
   c. penguins
6. A word in the story that goes with <u>tens</u> and <u>hundreds</u> is:
   a. largest
   b. thousands ✓
   c. October

★ Pretend you live on an ice island. On the back of this paper write about how you would live. What kind of house would you have? How about food and clothing?

Page 3

Name _____

Collecting Money

Would you like to collect coins? It's an interesting hobby and you can learn many things. Coins tell the history of a country. Some show pictures of famous people, rare birds and animals. There are buildings called mints in the United States where coins are made. Each mint places a special mark on coins <u>it</u> makes. Take good care of your coins; they are worth more if they look new. Maybe you'll be lucky and find a rare one.

1. In the story, the word <u>collect</u> means:
   a. bring together ✓
   b. take apart
   c. sharpen
2. Another word for <u>mark</u> is:
   a. make
   b. sign ✓
   c. part
3. The opposite of <u>interesting</u> is:
   a. dull ✓
   b. fun
   c. find
4. A word in the story that sounds like <u>maid</u> is:
   made
5. The word <u>It</u> stands for:
   a. the mint ✓
   b. coins
   c. birds
6. A word in the story that goes with <u>pennies</u> and <u>nickels</u> is:
   a. mark
   b. coins ✓
   c. people

★ On the back of this paper write about something you collect or would like to collect. Draw a picture to go with your story.

Page 4

Answer Key

Name _____

On a Starry Night

Long before movies or television, people looked at the stars at night. <u>They</u> gave names to groups of stars. One group of seven stars was called the Big Dipper. These stars form the shape of a cup with a long handle. The two large stars in front of the cup point to the north star. One star in the handle is a double star. When two stars circle each other they are known as a double star. Look at the night sky. Try to find the Big Dipper.

1. In the story, the word <u>handle</u> means:
   a. something on a plate
   b. something on a glass
   c. something on a cup

2. Another word for <u>find</u> is:
   a. lose
   b. discover
   c. hold

3. The opposite of <u>before</u> is:
   a. later
   b. today
   c. after

4. A word in the story that sounds like <u>inn</u> is:
   in

5. The word <u>they</u> stands for:
   a. people who lived long ago
   b. stars
   c. Big Dipper

6. A word in the story that goes with <u>sun</u> and <u>moon</u> is:
   a. shape
   b. stars
   c. handle

★ Imagine a group of stars. Draw a picture of them on the back of this paper. Write the name of your star group.

Page 5

Name _____

Talk to the Animals

For many years, scientists have studied how animals learn from one another. <u>They</u> have discovered many things. Birds, fish, monkeys, insects and other animals do talk to each other. They make signals that stand for danger and they can cry for help. They can tell others that food is waiting and where it is. Some animals do this by making sounds. Some move in a special way and some leave a scent trail. Watch some ants trail each other to a piece of candy. Rub your finger on the path. The scent trail is gone and the ants will scatter!

1. In the story, the word <u>discovered</u> means:
   a. played
   b. lost
   c. found out

2. Another word for <u>signals</u> is:
   a. flowers
   b. signs
   c. sugar

3. The opposite of <u>cry</u> is:
   a. laugh
   b. tap
   c. carry

4. A word in the story that sounds like <u>peace</u> is:
   piece

5. The word <u>they</u> stands for:
   a. animals
   b. scientists
   c. scent

6. A word in the story that goes with <u>smell</u> and <u>sniff</u> is:
   a. path
   b. scent
   c. piece

★ On the back of this paper write a story about animals who really talk. Tell what they might say.

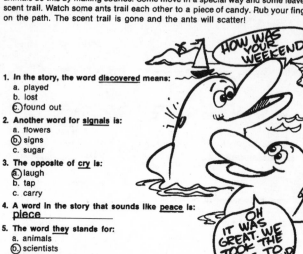

Page 6

Name _____

Where Does Cork Come From?

Have you ever wondered how a cork bottle stopper is made? Cork is the bark of the evergreen oak trees. These trees grow along the southern coast of Europe. Each time <u>their</u> bark is peeled, the oaks grow stronger and healthier. The cork is boiled to soften it, and then dried in sheets. Because it floats on water it is used to make life jackets. It is used to sound proof rooms because sound is trapped by cork. It can even be ground into cork flour and mixed with oil. This mixture is made into shiny floor coverings.

1. In the story, the word <u>cork</u> means:
   a. something that comes from flowers
   b. something that comes from animals
   c. something that comes from trees

2. Another word for <u>trapped</u> is:
   a. held
   b. played
   c. tossed

3. The opposite of <u>soften</u> is:
   a. shiny
   b. harden
   c. ribbon

4. A word in the story that sounds like <u>maid</u> is:
   made

5. The word <u>their</u> stands for:
   a. cork
   b. jackets
   c. trees

6. A word in the story that goes with <u>noise</u> and <u>clatter</u> is:
   a. rooms
   b. sound
   c. shiny

★ On the back of this paper make a list. Write everything you can think of that comes from trees. Draw some pictures to go with your list.

Page 7

Name _____   Date _____

The Case of the Halloween Trick

"What kind of Halloween is this?" asked Mr. Fletcher. "We give kids candy and then they steal tools from my garage." He called some of his neighbors to be on the lookout for a thief dressed as a trick-or-treater. A group of kids came to the door of the Billings house. Mrs. Billings answered the door. "What a cute costume," she told the clown, and tweaked his nose. He laughed. She yelled, "Boo!" at the ghost and he got scared. She pulled the hobo's beard and he yowled, "Ouch!" but the beard didn't come off. She jerked the devil's moustache and it fell off. "Don't leave yet, kids, the police are coming. One of you is not a child or trick-or-treater."

Who did it and how did Mrs. Billings know? _____
The hobo did it. Kids don't have real beards.

1. The main idea of this story is:
   a. a devil's moustache
   b. cute costumes
   c. a phony trick-or-treater

2. The ghost got scared because:
   a. Someone yelled at him.
   b. He looked in a mirror.
   c. Someone stepped on his sheet.

3. What happened to Mr. Fletcher?
   A thief stole his tools.

4. The thief probably thought:
   a. It was Christmas.
   b. He was pretty smart.
   c. Candy was awful.

5. The devil's moustache:
   a. got wet
   b. was sticky
   c. fell off

6. <u>Cute</u> means:
   a. charming or pretty
   b. bow-legged
   c. silly

Brainwork! On the back of this page, write a story about "The Best Halloween I Ever Had".

Page 8

FS-32045 Reading

Answer Key

The Case of the Classroom Cheater

"Scott! Shawn! Come here immediately!" demanded Mr. Doherty. The boys went up to the teacher's desk quietly. "Both of you got eighty-nine on the science test," said Mr. Doherty, "and you both got the same answers wrong. Neither of you knew in what year the telephone was invented." Scott said, "Mr. Doherty, I didn't cheat." Shawn looked insulted. "Well, I sure didn't cheat. I knew everything about Tom Edison and his telephone." Mr. Doherty shook his head. "I know who cheated," he said.

Who did it and how did Mr. Doherty know? **Shawn did it. He didn't know that Bell invented the telephone, but that wasn't the question he got wrong.**

1. The main idea of this story is:
   a. flunking a test
   (b.) a boy who cheated
   c. a great invention

2. Both boys:
   a. got all the questions right
   (b.) got the same score
   c. were brothers

3. Why did the teacher want to see the boys?
   One of them had cheated on a test.

4. You can tell that:
   a. Both boys lied.
   b. Kids always cheat.
   (c.) One of the boys lied.

5. What kind of test did the boys take?
   (a.) science   b. math   c. swimming

6. **Immediately** means:
   a. tomorrow
   b. yesterday
   (c.) right away

Brainwork! Think about the question and answer it on the back. What should Mr. Doherty do next?

Page 9

The Mystery of Mother's Note

Henry was in trouble again. His teacher, Ms. Haggerty, had given him a note to take home to his mother. The note said, "Dear Mrs. Simpson, Henry is failing all his subjects, especially spelling and math. He is not trying at all. Sincerely, Ms. Haggerty." Oh, boy, thought Henry. Am I going to get it! Hey! I'll write a different note. "Dear Mrs. Simpson, Henry is doing well in awl his subjects, expeciay speling and math." Henry gave the note to his mom. "Henry!" she yelled. "Wait until your father gets home. You wrote this note, not your teacher!"

How did Mrs. Simpson know that her son had written the note? **The note had misspelled words.**

1. The main idea of this story is:
   a. a good math student
   (b.) a boy in trouble
   c. a note for Father

2. How was Henry doing in school?
   a. very well
   b. pretty well
   (c.) very poorly

3. Which words in the note did Henry misspell? **awl (all), expeciay (especially), speling (spelling)**

4. You can tell that Henry thinks he is:
   (a.) pretty smart   b. very tall   c. a teacher

5. Henry decided to write:
   a. a Christmas card
   (b.) a different note
   c. a letter to his teacher

6. **Sincerely** means:
   a. happily
   b. sadly
   (c.) honestly

gulp!!!

Brainwork! Think about the question and answer it on the back. What should Henry tell his father when he gets home?

Page 10

The Case of the Missing Milk

Now for a glass of cold chocolate milk, thought Jason. He poured himself a full glass and had one gulp. Just then the phone rang. When Jason came back, the glass was empty! Maybe, he thought, his brother Toby drank it. Suddenly, Jason's cat, Muffin, ran across the room. She started to clean her whiskers, which looked brown. "Aha," Jason said out loud. "Muffin stuck her whole nose and mouth in my glass and drank all the milk! Muffin, why didn't you tell me you wanted some?" he laughed.

How did Jason know that Muffin had drunk his milk? **Her whiskers were brown from the chocolate milk.**

1. The main idea of this story is:
   (a.) a cat that liked milk
   b. a glass of water
   c. a phone call

2. Jason left his milk because:
   a. Muffin wanted her dinner.
   b. His mother wanted him.
   (c.) He heard the telephone.

3. At first, what did Jason think?
   He thought his brother drank the milk.

4. You can tell that:
   a. Jason shouted at Muffin.
   (b.) Jason wasn't angry.
   c. Jason's friend called.

5. How did Muffin's whiskers look?
   (a.) brown   b. stiff   c. gray

6. **Whiskers are:**
   a. milk on your face
   b. dirt on your face
   (c.) hair on your face

Brainwork! Think about the question and answer it on the back. How could you write this story with a different ending?

Page 11

The Case of the Missing Pearls

Nellie loved her new pearls. She wore them every day. At night she hid them in her sewing box. She thought that would be the last place that burglars would look. Aunt Jenny came to visit. She said she'd be glad to do some mending for Nellie. The next morning Nellie went to get her pearls. They were gone! Could the milkman or the plumber have taken them? Aunt Jenny came into the room. "Here's your dress that I mended, Nellie. It was missing some buttons, so I used those large white ones in your sewing box." Nellie screamed, "Oh, no!"

Who did it and how did Nellie know? **Aunt Jenny did it. She mended Nellie's dress. She thought the pearls were buttons.**

1. The main idea of this story is:
   a. a milkman
   b. a new dress
   (c.) a good place for pearls

2. Nellie didn't want burglars to:
   (a.) take her pearls
   b. stay for tea
   c. leave her house

3. What did Aunt Jenny want to do?
   Aunt Jenny wanted to mend Nellie's clothes.

4. You can tell that Aunt Jenny:
   a. is a plumber
   b. doesn't like to sew
   (c.) doesn't see too well

5. Nellie hid her pearls:
   a. all day
   (b.) at night
   c. in the attic

6. **Pearls are:**
   a. a kind of bird
   (b.) white gems made by oysters
   c. pieces of gold and silver

Brainwork! Think about the question and answer it on the back. What would be a better place to hide Nellie's pearls?

Page 12

Answer Key

Name _____ Date _____

The Case of the Missing Book

"Janice, will you read your book report first?" asked Mrs. Damon. Janice blushed. "I couldn't do it, Mrs. Damon. The book I chose, "A Horse of a Different Color," disappeared. I had it on my desk but someone took it." The kids took out their reports. Marvin's was about a lost dog. Miriam's was about a purple horse. Sally's was about a shipwrecked family named Robinson. Dana's was called "The Great Brain." Janice almost couldn't wait until the reports ended. She raised her hand. "Mrs. Damon, I know who took my book. Miriam did." Miriam said she was sorry. "I wanted to get that book, but you got it first," she said.

How did Janice know that Miriam had taken her book? __A purple horse__
__is a horse of a different color!__

1. **The main idea of this story is:**
   a. a purple cat
   b. book reports *(circled)*
   c. a lost dog

2. **Janice didn't do her report because:**
   a. Her book was gone. *(circled)*
   b. The teacher wouldn't let her.
   c. She didn't know how to read.

3. **Janice's book was called:**
   A Horse of a Different Color

4. **Janice's book was probably:**
   a. a true story
   b. a silly story *(circled)*
   c. a story about people

5. **Who reported on "The Great Brain"?**
   a. Janice
   b. Mrs. Damon
   c. Dana *(circled)*

6. **Blushed means:**
   a. turned white
   b. turned blue
   c. turned red *(circled)*

Brainwork! On the back of this page, write a story called "A Horse of a Different Color".

Page 13

Name _____ Date _____

The Case of the Broken Window

Mr. Phillips sat in his living room, reading his paper. Suddenly, there was a loud crash! A baseball came sailing through the window. Mr. Phillips took the ball and went outside. Some boys were playing in the street. "OK, who did it?" Mr. Phillips asked. "I didn't see it happen," said Bob. "Neither did I," said Sam. "I heard a noise," added Paul. "I wasn't near your living room," said Bill. "I don't play baseball," declared John. "I know who did it now," Mr. Phillips said.

Who did it and how did Mr. Phillips know? __Bill did it. Mr. Phillips never said the ball__
__had broken the living room window.__

1. **The main idea of this story is:**
   a. some noisy kids
   b. a baseball game
   c. the truth about a window *(circled)*

2. **Sam claimed that:**
   a. He didn't see the crime happen. *(circled)*
   b. He threw the baseball.
   c. He didn't know Mr. Phillips.

3. **What was Mr. Phillips doing?**
   Mr. Phillips was sitting in his living room, reading his paper.

4. **You can tell that Mr. Phillips:**
   a. was very happy
   b. felt angry *(circled)*
   c. threw the baseball himself

5. **Paul admitted he'd:**
   a. seen the whole thing
   b. gone to sleep
   c. heard a noise *(circled)*

6. **Frowning means:**
   a. smiling and cheering
   b. wrinkling your brow *(circled)*
   c. screaming out loud

Brainwork! Think about the question and answer it on the back.
What do you think Mr. Phillips should do about the person who broke his window?

Page 14

Name _____ Date _____

P.T. or Not P.T.?

The Andersons woke up late one Sunday morning. Cindy Anderson went outside. "Oh, no!" she yelled. Her parents came running. They gasped. Someone had covered their tree with rolls and rolls of paper towels! It had rained and now they were all stuck to the tree. Cindy called her friends. They were going shopping for their club picnic later. Alice would buy ketchup. Harriette listed fruit and milk. Sandra's list said hot dogs and six rolls of paper towels which her mother had asked her to get. Nora would buy the hot dog buns. "I know who messed up our tree," said Cindy.

Who did it and how did Cindy know? __Sandra did it. She'd used all her mother's__
__towels on the tree.__

1. **The main idea of this story is:**
   a. a long list
   b. a funny tree
   c. a mean trick *(circled)*

2. **During the night the towels got:**
   a. wet *(circled)*
   b. blown away
   c. dry

3. **What had happened to the tree?**
   Someone had covered it with rolls of paper towels.

4. **Cindy will probably:**
   a. laugh at the whole thing
   b. not want to be Sandra's friend *(circled)*
   c. tell her friends to go home

5. **Who would buy the hot dog buns?**
   a. Sandra
   b. Nora *(circled)*
   c. Cindy

6. **Gasped means:**
   a. to cry
   b. draw in the breath sharply *(circled)*
   c. to hold your breath for a long time

Brainwork! Think about the question and answer it on the back.
If a friend of yours "P.T.'d" your tree, what would you do?

Page 15

Name _____ Date _____

The Case of the Missing Flowers

"Allen Bloom!" yelled Mrs. Di Bento, Allen's neighbor. "I know you took my flowers. I never give them to anyone. You picked them!" Allen said he didn't, but Mrs. Di Bento wouldn't believe him. Just then, Mrs. Di Bento's son, Darrell, came home from school. A note was in his hand. It fell to the ground. Allen picked it up. It said, Dear Mrs. Di Bento, Thank you for the flowers, Signed, Mrs. Lovelady, Darrell's teacher. "Darrell took your flowers," said Allen. "I'm sorry I accused you," blushed Mrs. Di Bento.

How did Allen know that Darrell took the flowers? __Darrell's teacher wrote a__
__thank you note for the flowers.__

1. **The main idea of this story is:**
   a. daisies and pansies
   b. falsely accused *(circled)*
   c. a blushing neighbor

2. **Darrell was carrying:**
   a. a bunch of flowers
   b. a thank-you note *(circled)*
   c. his report card

3. **Of what did Mrs. Di Bento accuse Allen?**
   Mrs. Di Bento accused Allen of taking her flowers.

4. **You can tell that Darrell:**
   a. wanted to make his mother mad
   b. wanted to get Allen in trouble
   c. wanted to please his teacher *(circled)*

5. **Mrs. Di Bento was:**
   a. Darrell's neighbor
   b. Allen's sister
   c. Allen's neighbor *(circled)*

6. **Accuse means:**
   a. saying someone did something *(circled)*
   b. yelling at someone
   c. calling the police

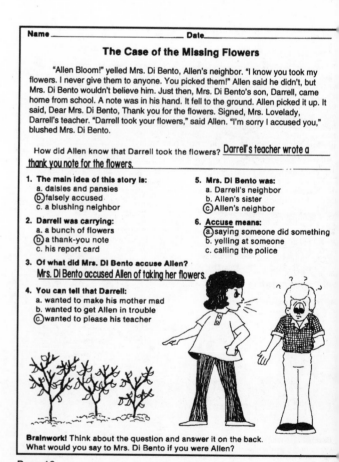

Brainwork! Think about the question and answer it on the back.
What would you say to Mrs. Di Bento if you were Allen?

Page 16

FS-32045 Reading

Answer Key

Name _____ Date _____

Curlock Soams and the Pilfered Pie

Curlock Soams and Dr. Spotson were eating at Pierre's Place, a famous restaurant. "And now, Mr. Soams," beamed Pierre, "my specialty, pickled prune pie." Pierre lifted the lid on the pie plate. "It is gone!" he shrieked, fainting with a thud on the floor. "None of you chaps leave the room," ordered Curlock. "Who else had this dessert tonight?" Pierre sighed, sitting up. "I prepared it just for you." Soams looked around. The customers at table two had yellow stains on their ties. Another customer was wiping whipped cream off her face. The man at table five put his black-stained handkerchief back into his pocket. "Aha," said Soams. "I've done it again."

Who did it and how did Soams know? __The man at table five did it.__
__Prunes are black and he had black stains on his handkerchief.__

1. The main idea of this story is:
a. a man who fainted
b. a missing pie ⓑ
c. whipped cream and pie

2. What was in the pie plate?
a. cream pie
b. pumpkin pie
ⓒ nothing

3. When Pierre saw the empty pie plate he
__fainted on the floor.__

4. You can tell that Curlock is:
a. very fond of pie
b. a good detective ⓑ
c. a great cook

5. What was Pierre's specialty?
ⓐ pickled prune pie
b. pecan pie
c. pelican pie

6. Pilfered means:
a. eaten   ⓑ stolen   c. broken

Brainwork! On the back of this page, make up a silly kind of pie and list what would be in it.

Page 17

Name _____ Date _____

The Case of the Missing Sandwich

Sara brought her favorite lunch to school today. It is a peanut butter and banana sandwich. She wouldn't tell any of her friends what she had. They would all want a bite. At lunch, Sara excitedly opened her lunch box. Hey! Tuna! Someone had switched sandwiches! Sara said, "Someone took my sandwich and I don't like tuna!" Her friends said they were sorry. Kevin said, "Who would want peanut butter and banana, anyway?" Sara jumped up. "You took it, Kevin!" Kevin told Sara he would bring her a new sandwich tomorrow.

How did Sara know that Kevin had taken her sandwich? _____
__No one else knew what kind of sandwich she'd brought.__

1. The main idea of this story is:
a. a tuna sandwich
b. late for lunch
ⓒ switching sandwiches

2. With whom did Sara eat lunch?
a. her teacher
b. her brother
ⓒ some friends

3. What kind of sandwich did Sara like?
__Sara liked a peanut butter and banana sandwich.__

4. Kevin probably:
a. wanted to be mean
ⓑ wanted to try the sandwich
c. didn't like sandwiches

5. Sara thought her friends:
ⓐ would want a bite
b. would want to play
c. like to take things

6. Switched means:
a. to keep
ⓑ to exchange
c. to eat

Brainwork! Think about the question and answer it on the back. Why do you think Kevin didn't just ask Sara to share her sandwich?

Page 18

Name _____ Date _____

The Case of the Missing Dog

The phone rang loudly. Curlock Soams grouchily rose from his comfy chair. "Hello! Mr. Soams!" came a panicky voice over the phone. "My valuable dog has been stolen!" It was Curlock's neighbor, Mrs. Broomhead. The detective sprang into action. No one in the neighborhood but Mrs. Broomhead had a dog. Curlock walked around the block. Mrs. Singer had cans of cat food falling out of her garbage cans. Poor Mr. Dingman had a mess in his driveway. Dog food was falling out of a big sack. The Robinsons had sacks of birdseed near their side door. "By Jove!" shouted Curlock. "I've cracked the case."

Who did it and how did Curlock know? __Mr. Dingman did it.__
__He didn't have a dog but had dog food.__

1. The main idea of this story is:
a. a grouchy detective
b. finding a dognapper ⓑ
c. eating birdseed

2. What was Curlock doing?
a. feeding his cat
b. playing his violin
ⓒ sitting in a chair

3. Who had a mess in his driveway?
__Mr. Dingman had a messy driveway.__

4. You can tell that the dognapper:
ⓐ lived in the neighborhood
b. was a bird
c. had a pet shop

5. Curlock decided to:
a. take a dog
b. take a walk ⓑ
c. take a nap

6. Panicky means:
ⓐ terrified
b. itchy
c. funny

Brainwork! Think about the question and answer it on the back. Why would someone take a dog?

Page 19

Name _____ Date _____

The Case of the Vicious Vandals

Some awful people had broken into the school. There was damage to some classrooms and things were missing. Two typewriters had been taken from the office. Mrs. Loomis, the school secretary, said one of the typewriters had a broken key. "The C key is broken and all the C's look like G's." Mr. Chester's English class was getting ready to turn in their stories. "Pass them all in, please," asked the teacher. He looked them over. "I noticed that some people typed their stories. Susan, yours, "The Cat and the Dog," is very neat. Gary, "The Gat and the Garrot" is unusual. Harold, "The Broken Umbrella" looks great. By the way, I know who one of the vandals is."

Who did it and how did the teacher know? __Gary did it. His typewriter__
__key was broken the same as the one which was stolen.__
__His title should have read "The Cat & the Carrot".__

1. The main idea of this story is:
ⓐ finding the vandal
b. a broken umbrella
c. an English class

2. Mr. Chester asked his class to:
a. type their papers
b. go to recess
ⓒ turn in their papers

3. Two typewriters were
__missing.__

4. You can tell that one of the vandals:
a. was a fifth grader
ⓑ was in English class
c. was laughing

5. The school was broken into:
a. on Friday
b. by girls
ⓒ by awful people

6. Vandals are people who:
a. rob banks
ⓑ destroy property
c. clean schools

Brainwork! Think about the question and answer it on the back. What do you think should be done about vandals?

Page 20

Answer Key

Name_____ Date_____

The Case of the Missing Piece

"Ready for the Monopoly game?" asked Anita. "OK," said Alfie. They took out the set. "My favorite piece is this tiny blue truck," said Alfie. "Mine is the little pair of scissors," said Anita, "but it seems to be gone. Who took it?" Anita's other brother, Algie, was crying in the next room. "Mom, will you please tell him to be quiet?" asked Anita. "He's only two, Anita," said her mother, "and I told him he's too small to cut paper. Now he insists he has something special and won't hurt himself." Anita smiled. "I think I solved my mystery," she said.

Who did it and how did Anita know? **Algie did it.**
The "something special" was the missing game piece.

1. The main idea of this story is:
   a. a small blue truck
   b. a noisy brother
   c. a missing pair of scissors

2. The pair of scissors was:
   a. big
   b. not in the game box
   c. left outside

3. Anita's brothers were named
   Alfie and Algie.

4. You can tell that:
   a. Algie is older than Anita.
   b. Anita's mother likes Monopoly.
   c. Algie is the youngest.

5. Anita wanted her brother to be:
   a. gone
   b. quiet
   c. tall

6. A favorite is:
   a. the one you like best
   b. the one you don't like
   c. the one you break

Brainwork! Think about the question and answer it on the back.
What will happen when Algie tries to cut with his "special scissors"?

Page 21

Name_____ Date_____

The Case of the Missing Pencil

"Oh, no!" shouted Pamela. "Someone took my red pencil. I'm the only one in the class who has one. All of you have green pencils." No one admitted taking the pencil. Pamela borrowed a pencil from Grace. "Adam, please bring me a piece of green drawing paper," asked Mrs. Fisk. When Adam brought the paper, the teacher smiled. "I forgot that you're color blind, Adam. That paper is red." Suddenly, Pamela jumped up. "Adam took my pencil, but I'm sure it was a mistake. Sure, here it is on his desk." Adam looked puzzled.

How did Pamela know Adam had taken her pencil? **Mrs. Fisk said**
Adam was color blind. He thought the red pencil was
really green.

1. The main idea of this story is:
   a. a big pencil
   b. taken by mistake
   c. a nice teacher

2. Adam brought Mrs. Fisk
   a. the wrong color paper
   b. a blue pencil
   c. his math paper

3. Pamela borrowed a pencil from
   Grace.

4. You can tell that Adam:
   a. always took pencils
   b. yelled at Pamela
   c. didn't know he had the red pencil

5. Mrs. Fisk had forgotten:
   a. her car keys
   b. that Adam wasn't smart
   c. that Adam was color blind

6. Denied means:
   a. said something wasn't true
   b. hurt his knee
   c. stole something

Brainwork! Think about the question and answer it on the back.
How could Adam keep from mistaking red pencils for green ones?

Page 22

Name_____ Date_____

The Case of the Missing Lunch Money

Mrs. Kimball had told her class never to leave money in their desks. Carl's mother had given him a ten-dollar bill and told him to bring her the change. Carl put the money in his desk. At lunchtime, he reached into the desk. He came up with a piece of paper that said, "Thanks for the money." Carl stood up and yelled, "My money is gone!" Mrs. Kimball asked, "Did anyone see Carl's money? I won't say how much is missing." Annie said, "I found a dime today." Jane added, "Maybe he lost his money." Arnold said, "He shouldn't have brought ten dollars to school." Pete said, "Ten dollars? Wow!" Mrs. Kimball frowned. "I know who took the money."

Who did it and how did the teacher know? **Arnold did it. He was**
the only one who knew the amount Carl had.

1. The main idea of this story is:
   a. finding a quarter
   b. a careless boy
   c. an angry mother

2. Carl knew his mother would be:
   a. happy
   b. funny
   c. angry

3. What had Carl taken to school?
   Carl had taken a ten-dollar bill.

4. You can tell that Carl was:
   a. careful b. laughing c. careless

5. Carl left his money in his:
   a. shoe
   b. desk
   c. wallet

6. Frowned means:
   a. smile
   b. bring your brows together
   c. sniff in the air

Brainwork! Think about the question and answer it on the back.
What should Carl have done to make sure no one took his money?

Page 23

Name_____ Date_____

The Case of the Ghostly Visit

Jack and Beatrice had bet their friends that they would go to the old Bramble house. Everyone knew the place was haunted. Jack and Beatrice entered the house. The door creaked and there were spiderwebs all over the place. Suddenly, a white figure jumped out and yelled, "Boo! Leave my house, you two!" The kids ran screaming all the way home. The next day was windy. All the neighbors' clothing was hanging on lines, drying in the breeze. Jimmy Jones' lines had lots of diapers on them. Sam Silver's had lots of sheets. One of them needed patching because it had two large holes in it. Susan Small's line had tiny doll clothes on it. Beatrice and Jack looked at each other. They knew the ghost's secret.

Who did it and how did the kids know? **Sam did it.**
The holes in the sheet were the "ghosts" eyeholes.

1. The main idea of this story is:
   a. finding a ghost
   b. a stiff wind
   c. creaking doors and spiderwebs

2. The ghost told the kids to:
   a. make him a sandwich
   b. close the door
   c. get out of the house

3. Where were Jack and Beatrice going?
   They were going to a haunted house.

4. You can tell that the kids:
   a. weren't scared at all
   b. really were scared
   c. loved ghosts

5. What was hanging on lines?
   a. telephones
   b. clothes
   c. pictures

6. Figure means:
   a. ghost b. shape c. house

Brainwork! On the back of this page, write a ghost story in two paragraphs.

Page 24

110

FS-32045 Readin

Answer Key

The Case of the Ruined Birthday

World-famous detective Curlock Soams was getting ready for his niece Bridget's surprise birthday party. Suddenly, there was a knock at the door. "Curlock!" yelled his sister. "The cake I made is missing! All six layers of it! The birthday is ruined!" "Not to worry, my dear. Spotson and I will solve this case." Curlock was soon joined by his able assistant, Dr. Spotson. "I do have an idea, Spotson," said Curlock. "Let's go to Barker's Bakery." Spotson was puzzled. "But Curlock, they have awful cakes." "Oh, Mr. Soams," said Barker. "I hear your niece is having a birthday. I just happen to have a birthday cake all ready." "Just a minute, Barker," frowned Curlock. "You stole my niece's cake and now you want to sell it back to me."

How did Curlock know Mr. Barker did it? **No one knew about the birthday because it was a surprise. Mr. Barker wouldn't have known they needed a cake.**

1. The main idea of this story is:
   a. a bad baker
   b. a missing cake ✓
   c. a great party

2. Soams knew he could:
   a. find the answer ✓
   b. sing "Happy Birthday"
   c. eat some cake

3. Who joined Curlock?
   Dr. Spotson joined Curlock.

4. You can tell that:
   a. Curlock likes chocolate.
   b. Bridget is ten years old.
   c. Curlock is very helpful. ✓

5. Barker's cakes were:
   a. delicious
   b. awful ✓
   c. gone

6. An **assistant** is:
   a. a cake
   b. a boss
   c. a helper ✓

Brainwork! Think about the question and answer it on the back. What did Curlock do after he found the cake thief?

The Case of the April Fool's Joke

"Look out, everyone," warned Mr. Jenkins. "Today is April Fool's Day. I hope that no one will play jokes that are mean." Later that day, the joke was on Mr. Jenkins. As he sat down, he slid right onto the floor. "Someone put oil on that chair. Now my pants have an oil stain, and that's very hard to get out." Later, Mr. Jenkins called on some students to do math problems. Alma had eaten a jelly sandwich for lunch. She left some jelly on the board. "Will the board monitor please wipe off the board?" asked the teacher. Tommy did his job but his hand left a big, greasy mark on the board. "Now, that's worse," said Mr. Jenkins, "but I have solved the mystery of the April Fool's joke."

Whodunit and how did Mr. Jenkins know? **Tommy did it. Since he left a greasy mark, he'd been handling oil.**

1. The main idea of this story is:
   a. a board with jelly
   b. a mean joke ✓
   c. a teacher that got hurt

2. What happened to Mr. Jenkins?
   a. He fell out of his chair. ✓
   b. He got jelly on his chin.
   c. He fell and cried.

3. What did Tommy leave on the board?
   a greasy mark

4. Mr. Jenkins probably felt:
   a. happy   b. angry ✓   c. mean

5. What did Alma leave on the board?
   a. the chalk
   b. a math problem
   c. some jelly ✓

6. A **stain** is:
   a. a kind of meat
   b. a spot ✓
   c. a country in Europe

Brainwork! Think about the question and answer it on the back. Make a list of April Fool's jokes you'd like to play.

The Greatest

Muhammad Ali was the first heavyweight boxing **champion** to win the **title** three times. He was one of the most interesting stars in sports. Muhammad called himself "The Greatest".

Muhammad Ali became famous after he won a Gold Medal in the Olympic Games of 1960. Besides boxing, Ali has written a book about himself. He also wrote funny **poems** which teased the people he boxed. Sometimes he acted on TV and in movies.

Spending his time helping children is important to Ali. He tells them that if they try hard they can do well in life, too. In 1978 Muhammad lost his title. Later that year he got it back. In 1979 Muhammad Ali retired from boxing, still the champ.

1. The main idea of this story is:
   a. Muhammad Ali was a real champion. ✓
   b. Boxing is fun.
   c. Muhammad Ali writes poems.

2. Muhammad says:
   a. He can play baseball.
   b. He is great. ✓
   c. People tease him.

3. When did Muhammad Ali become famous?
   a. when he was a baby
   b. when he wrote a book
   c. after the Olympic Games ✓

4. What word means to make fun of, to laugh at someone?
   a. title
   b. tease ✓
   c. box

5. The story doesn't say, but Muhammad Ali probably:
   a. trained very hard to become a good boxer ✓
   b. likes ice cream and cake
   c. is very skinny

Stars from the Good Old Days

The picture on TV looks kind of fuzzy. Don't try to fix it! This show was made in the 1930's. The film is very old. The "Little **Rascals**" you see on TV used to be called "The Our Gang **Comedies**".

The Rascals were a group of kids. They did funny things and got into trouble. They had funny names, too. **Alfalfa** was tall and skinny. He tried to be very serious. Spanky was chubby with a funny voice. Darla was the only girl member of the gang. Even today, these kids and their mischief are fun to watch.

Stan **Laurel** and **Oliver** Hardy also made movies in the 1930's and 1940's. Oliver, tall and fat, always picked on Laurel, the skinny one. Sometimes Laurel made Hardy look silly. They did things like trip each other and fall down. Sometimes they'd get pies thrown in their faces. More than forty years later, they still make us laugh.

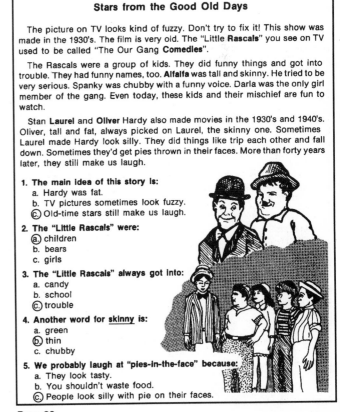

1. The main idea of this story is:
   a. Hardy was fat.
   b. TV pictures sometimes look fuzzy.
   c. Old-time stars still make us laugh. ✓

2. The "Little Rascals" were:
   a. children ✓
   b. bears
   c. girls

3. The "Little Rascals" always got into:
   a. candy
   b. school
   c. trouble ✓

4. Another word for **skinny** is:
   a. green
   b. thin ✓
   c. chubby

5. We probably laugh at "pies-in-the-face" because:
   a. They look tasty.
   b. You shouldn't waste food.
   c. People look silly with pie on their faces. ✓

Answer Key

Comic Book Heroes

You know Superman, Batman, Wonder Woman and Spiderman. They've all been on TV. Superman even had a movie made about his life. Don't forget "The **Incredible** Hulk", either.

All these "super heroes" are fun to see. Superman can fly. Batman and Robin have so many tricks. Wonder Woman has magic **bracelets** and a rope. They protect her and help catch bad guys, too. Spiderman is amazing. He can climb up buildings. And the Hulk is so strong!

These famous heroes started out in comic books. People liked their adventures very much. Television shows were made about them. Sometimes they seem very real. We even know the story of Superman's whole life. It would be fun to see him really speeding through the sky!

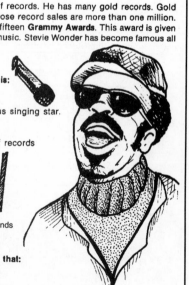

1. **The main idea of this story is:**
   a. about super heroes *(circled)*
   b. about comic books
   c. climbing up buildings
2. **Wonder Woman's bracelets:**
   a. help keep her safe *(circled)*
   b. are gold
   c. look nice
3. **The super heroes started out in:**
   a. movies
   b. radio
   c. comic books *(circled)*
4. **A hulk is:**
   a. a green plant
   b. a forest animal
   c. a big, clumsy person *(circled)*
5. **Super heroes probably:**
   a. always win *(circled)*
   b. never win
   c. are crybabies

Page 29

A Man Who Cared

Roberto Clemente was born in Puerto Rico. When he was young he came to the United States. When he grew up he became one of the best baseball players ever.

Roberto won four batting **titles**. He played on twelve all-star teams. In 197? he was named the best player in the World Series. He was the eleventh man in history to get 3,000 hits.

Roberto played baseball for eighteen happy years. But he cared about people, too. In 1972 a strong **earthquake** hit the country of **Nicaragua**. Many people were killed or left homeless. Roberto wanted to help. He flew to Nicaragua. On the way there, his plane crashed and he was killed. Roberto Clemente was a great ball player and a great person.

1. **The main idea of this story is:**
   a. Roberto Clemente was a great person. *(circled)*
   b. Many people got 3,000 hits.
   c. Baseball players are nice.
2. **Roberto Clemente:**
   a. wanted to be a farmer
   b. liked helping people *(circled)*
   c. played soccer
3. **Roberto was born in:**
   a. New York
   b. California
   c. Puerto Rico *(circled)*
4. **An earthquake is:**
   a. movement of the earth *(circled)*
   b. a big storm
   c. the sound a duck makes
5. **You can tell that Roberto Clemente:**
   a. wanted to stop playing baseball
   b. liked playing baseball *(circled)*
   c. was six feet tall

Page 30

A Musical Wonder

He sings rock and other **music**. He writes his own songs and plays many **instruments**. Stevie Wonder does these things very well. Yet he has been blind all his life.

Stevie has been able to overcome his blindness. He wrote and recorded his first song at age twelve. At that time Stevie's songs were very lively. Stevie also writes serious songs.

Stevie's songs sell millions of records. He has many gold records. Gold records are given to people whose record sales are more than one million. Stevie has also won more than fifteen **Grammy Awards**. This award is given for writing, singing or playing music. Stevie Wonder has become famous all over the world.

1. **The main idea of this story is:**
   a. People buy records.
   b. Children write songs.
   c. Stevie Wonder is a famous singing star. *(circled)*
2. **Gold records are given:**
   a. to dairy farmers
   b. for songs that sell lots of records *(circled)*
   c. to movie stars
3. **Stevie writes his own:**
   a. books
   b. letters
   c. songs *(circled)*
4. **Music means:**
   a. a pleasing combination of sounds *(circled)*
   b. a kind of paper
   c. a person
5. **From this story you can tell that:**
   a. Stevie loves music. *(circled)*
   b. Stevie is six feet tall.
   c. Stevie was born in Michigan.

Page 31

Kermit, Miss Piggy and Friends

Kermit the Frog and Miss Piggy seem like real people. So do the rest of that **gang** called "The **Muppets**". Jim Henson started the Muppets in the 1950's. It was a new idea in puppets. Some Muppets are small and some are as large as real people. The Muppets stand on a stage and are moved from below. Each Muppet is worked by a different person.

Kermit and Miss Piggy are the most famous Muppets. Miss Piggy thinks she's beautiful. She wants people to **admire** her. Kermit was the first Muppet. Jim Henson was the voice of Kermit. Miss Piggy always runs after Kermit.

The muppets became so famous they had a TV show and made movies.

1. **The main idea of this story is:**
   a. Miss Piggy is pretty.
   b. Kermit is green.
   c. The Muppets are big stars. *(circled)*
2. **The Muppets are worked by:**
   a. two people who hop around a lot
   b. many different people *(circled)*
   c. elves who live under the stage
3. **The man who started the Muppets was:**
   a. Jim Henson *(circled)*
   b. Kermit the Frog
   c. George Washington
4. **Famous means:**
   a. liking cookies
   b. being known by many people *(circled)*
   c. blowing up balloons
5. **The Muppets are probably well-liked because:**
   a. They're all different colors.
   b. People like pigs.
   c. They are funny. *(circled)*

Page 32

112

Answer Key

Name _____ Date _____

Marathon Man

Children run every day at home and at school. But what is it like to run in a marathon race? It's 26 miles of running without stopping. Thousands of men and women run to beat you, too. In the 1960's people began jogging. By the 1970's everyone got faster! Running became a big sport. Now cities all over America have races. Some are short, only ten **kilometers**. Others, like those in Boston and New York, are marathons.

Bill Rodgers has been in many marathons. In 1979 he won his fourth New York Marathon. More than 11,000 people ran against him! Bill ran the 26 miles in 2 hours, 11 minutes and 42 seconds.

Bill Rodgers has also won the Boston Marathon and many others. Running is a good sport. All you need are good running shoes and comfortable clothes.

1. **The main idea of this story is:**
   a. good running shoes
   b. about Boston and New York
   c. about running and Bill Rodgers

2. **Marathon running is done by:**
   a. many people
   b. women only
   c. a few people

3. **By 1979 how many New York Marathons had Bill Rodgers won?**
   a. 10
   b. 2
   c. 4

4. **A kilometer is:**
   a. a kind of measurement
   b. a kind of shoe
   c. a kind of sport

5. **In order to win a marathon race, you should:**
   a. practice running long distances
   b. buy some running shorts
   c. watch lots of TV

Page 33

Name _____ Date _____

One Giant Step for Mankind

Imagine being the first person to set foot on the moon! Neil **Armstrong** was the lucky one! In 1969, **astronauts** Armstrong and Edwin E. Aldrin, Jr., landed on the moon. They gathered dirt and rocks. **Millions** of people saw it on TV.

Going to the moon wasn't Neil's first time in space. In 1969 he and David Scott had docked two ships in space for the first time. While they were aboard, one ship began to shake. But they knew what they were doing. They stopped the shaking and landed safely.

The first moon landing was very important. We found out what the moon was made of. The flight proved that we could visit other planets. Neil Armstrong was a real space **pioneer**.

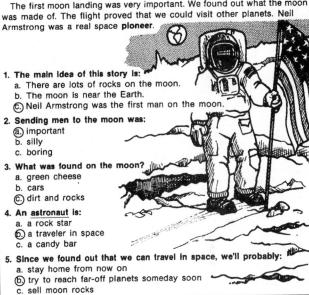

1. **The main idea of this story is:**
   a. There are lots of rocks on the moon.
   b. The moon is near the Earth.
   c. Neil Armstrong was the first man on the moon.

2. **Sending men to the moon was:**
   a. important
   b. silly
   c. boring

3. **What was found on the moon?**
   a. green cheese
   b. cars
   c. dirt and rocks

4. **An astronaut is:**
   a. a rock star
   b. a traveler in space
   c. a candy bar

5. **Since we found out that we can travel in space, we'll probably:**
   a. stay home from now on
   b. try to reach far-off planets someday soon
   c. sell moon rocks

Page 34

Name _____ Date _____

"Heyyy, It's the Fonz!"

The Fonz comes into the soda shop. He snaps his fingers and music comes from the **jukebox**. Everyone likes the Fonz. He's always around when needed.

The real name of the Fonz is Arthur **Fonzarelli**, but his friends call him "the Fonz" or "Fonzie". He fixes cars better than anyone. His best friends, the **Cunninghams**, treat him like one of the family. Fonzie pretends to be tough, but he is really kind and gentle.

The actor who played Fonzie on the show "Happy Days" is Henry **Winkler**. Henry also plays many other roles in movies and TV. He does other things, too. Henry tells people about special children. Many of these children can't walk, see or hear. But they like to play and have fun, too. Henry Winkler cares about people. He is just as nice as the Fonz.

1. **The main idea of this story is:**
   a. about Henry Winkler
   b. TV shows
   c. things children can do

2. **The Fonz likes to:**
   a. help people
   b. eat candy
   c. sing songs

3. **Who does Henry Winkler tell people about?**
   a. whales
   b. special children
   c. truck drivers

4. **A jukebox is:**
   a. a package
   b. a kind of snake
   c. a big record player

5. **The story doesn't tell:**
   a. what Fonzie wears
   b. Fonzie's real name
   c. the name of Fonzie's friends

Page 35

Name _____ Date _____

An American Hero

John **Wayne** made more than 175 movies in his life. The first time he was in a movie was in 1928. But John didn't become famous until 1939. After that, whenever someone needed a cowboy star, he was called. He also made many war and police movies.

People all over the world thought of John Wayne as a hero. He **reminded** them of all the good things about Americans. Some Americans became angry with John Wayne, though. He felt that Americans should fight the war in **Vietnam**. Many people didn't agree. But they knew he was brave to speak his mind.

John Wayne won an "Oscar" for being the best actor of 1969. In 1979, just before he died, he was given a medal. The United States gives this medal to people who serve their country well.

1. **The main idea of this story is:**
   a. Cowboys like horses.
   b. Oscars are given to good actors.
   c. John Wayne was liked by many people.

2. **People felt that John Wayne:**
   a. was a good American
   b. shouldn't have made movies
   c. was a good swimmer

3. **John Wayne starred in:**
   a. cowboy movies
   b. musical movies
   c. movies about animals

4. **Reminded means:**
   a. to babysit
   b. to make someone remember
   c. to listen carefully

5. **From the story you can tell that:**
   a. Movie stars like to be cowboys.
   b. John Wayne was proud to be an American.
   c. Movies are hard to make.

Page 36

113

Answer Key

Everybody Loves Lucy

It's time for "I Love Lucy". Every day millions of people watch **Lucille Ball** on television. But this show was first shown on TV in 1951!

Children still love Lucy although these old shows aren't even in color. Lucy is funny. Strange and **amusing** things always happen to her. She's always getting herself in trouble.

Lucille Ball began acting in the movies in the 1930's. She was in plays, too. At first she didn't do funny parts. Then people found out she could make them laugh. Lucy and her husband were given their own TV show. People like to watch Lucy, her family and their neighbors. Fifty years from now "I Love Lucy" will probably still be on TV!

1. **The main idea of this story is:**
   a. "Lucy" isn't in color.
   b. TV shows are funny.
   c. "Lucy" is a show people like. ✓

2. **Lucille Ball was good at:**
   a. playing baseball
   b. doing funny things on TV ✓
   c. knitting

3. **What always happens on "I Love Lucy"?**
   a. Lucy gets into trouble. ✓
   b. Lucy goes to school.
   c. Lucy goes to the store.

4. **Amusing means:**
   a. feeling sad
   b. something funny ✓
   c. being mean

5. **You can guess that:**
   a. "Lucy" is on late at night.
   b. "Lucy" is a police show.
   c. Lucille Ball liked to make people laugh. ✓

Page 37

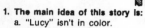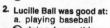

Soccer Champ

Pelé was known as the world's best soccer player. He was born to a poor family in **Brazil**. Like most people in his country, he loves soccer. He was such a good player that he became rich and famous. Pelé proved that a person from a poor family can **succeed**. Everyone in Brazil is very proud of him.

Pelé played on three world **championship** teams. He **retired** in 1974. Then he came to America. In 1977 Pelé led his new team, the New York Cosmos, to a championship. After that he retired for good.

Pelé is still famous, though. The whole world knows who he is. It will be a long time before anyone takes Pelé's place in soccer.

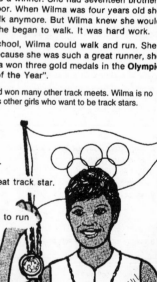

1. **The main idea of this story is:**
   a. Soccer is a good sport.
   b. Pelé was a great soccer player. ✓
   c. Playing soccer makes you rich.

2. **Soccer in Brazil:**
   a. is played by poor people only
   b. is played by many bad players
   c. is very well-liked ✓

3. **Why did Pelé come to America?**
   a. to see New York
   b. to play soccer ✓
   c. to sing

4. **To retire in this story means:**
   a. to work hard
   b. to put new tires on your car
   c. to stop working ✓

5. **How do soccer fans probably feel about Pelé?**
   a. They think he's the greatest. ✓
   b. They don't know who he is.
   c. They don't like him.

Page 38

The First Home Run King

The first great home run hitter in baseball was George **Herman** Ruth. Everyone called him "Babe". Babe started out as a pitcher. Soon it was discovered that he was even better as a hitter. Before Babe's time, players did not hit home runs very often. Babe made baseball more exciting by hitting "homers". Soon other players began trying to hit the ball as far as Babe did.

Babe Ruth joined the New York **Yankees** in 1920. Many people came to the games just to see him play. Soon Yankee **Stadium** was called "The House that Ruth Built".

In his life Babe hit 714 home runs. It was 40 years before this home run record was broken! Babe retired in 1935. The next year he was chosen for the **National** Baseball Hall of Fame.

1. **The main idea of this story is:**
   a. "Babe" is a strange name.
   b. Baseball is played in Yankee Stadium.
   c. Babe Ruth was a great baseball player. ✓

2. **Babe Ruth:**
   a. made people want to watch the Yankees ✓
   b. liked cars
   c. was a great skater

3. **Babe was chosen for:**
   a. bubble gum cards
   b. the Hall of Fame ✓
   c. movie star of the year

4. **To be chosen is to:**
   a. be fat
   b. be good
   c. be picked ✓

5. **From the story you cannot tell:**
   a. how many home runs Babe Ruth hit
   b. what team Babe played with
   c. the color of Babe's baseball suit ✓

Page 39

The Runner Who Couldn't Walk

Wilma **Rudolph** didn't start out as a winner. She had seventeen brothers and sisters. Her family was very poor. When Wilma was four years old she became very sick. She couldn't walk anymore. But Wilma knew she would walk again. Slowly and painfully she began to walk. It was hard work.

By the time she reached high school, Wilma could walk and run. She played basketball and ran track. Because she was such a great runner, she got to go to **college**. In 1960, Wilma won three gold medals in the **Olympic** Games. She was named "Athlete of the Year".

After the Olympics, Wilma entered and won many other track meets. Wilma is no longer entering meets herself. She helps other girls who want to be track stars.

1. **The main idea of this story is:**
   a. Sometimes people can't walk.
   b. Wilma Rudolph is a coach.
   c. Wilma Rudolph became a great track star. ✓

2. **Wilma**
   a. owns a store
   b. helps other people who want to run ✓
   c. teaches reading

3. **Wilma won:**
   a. a blue ribbon
   b. a new car
   c. gold medals ✓

4. **Track is a sport in which you:**
   a. swim
   b. run as fast as you can ✓
   c. race cars

5. **By learning to walk and run again, Wilma showed:**
   a. She was brave. ✓
   b. She was silly.
   c. She was lazy.

Page 40

Answer Key

Music for Everyone

Arthur **Fiedler** was a fine conductor. He started out by playing the **violin** in **orchestras**. His name even means "fiddler". In 1930 he was made conductor of the Boston Pops Orchestra. He conducted **concerts** until his death in 1979 at the age of 84.

Arthur Fiedler was different from other conductors. He knew that many people didn't like "serious" music. So Arthur decided to play the kind of music everyone would like. He played dance music and rock. He played the songs of the Beatles. He played music from shows and movies. Soon Arthur's music was even on TV. His program was called, "Evening at the Pops".

Arthur wanted people to buy his records, too. On the record covers he often dressed in costumes. Once he was Santa Claus. Another time he was Yankee Doodle Dandy. Arthur Fiedler said that all he wanted to do was to give people a good time.

1. **The main idea of this story is:**
   a. about orchestras
   b. about Arthur Fiedler
   c. about dance music

2. **Arthur Fiedler conducted:**
   a. trains
   b. music that many people liked
   c. only violin music

3. **Arthur's orchestra was called:**
   a. The Boston Pops
   b. The Boston Bulldogs
   c. The Boston Tea Party

4. **During a concert:**
   a. You see a movie.
   b. A team plays football.
   c. You listen to people playing or singing music.

5. **You can tell that:**
   a. Arthur Fiedler hated music.
   b. Arthur knew what people liked.
   c. Arthur was born in 1950.

Page 41

"What's Up, Doc?"

Bugs Bunny runs across the screen. Elmer Fudd is chasing him. "Come back here, Wabbit!" Bugs answers, "Sorry, Doc, but I don't feel like being your dinner." In the next **cartoon**, Daffy Duck is in trouble as usual.

If you close your eyes, you know who each cartoon star is. Each of their voices is different. But guess what? All these voices were done by one man.

Mel Blanc was the voice of the Roadrunner, Wiley **Coyote** and many other cartoon **favorites**. You never saw Mel's face. But the voices he did were famous all over the world.

1. **The main idea of this story is:**
   a. how cartoons are made
   b. the many voices of Mel Blanc
   c. a famous rabbit

2. **Elmer likes to:**
   a. run after Bugs Bunny
   b. catch chickens
   c. play tennis

3. **Mel Blanc was the voice of:**
   a. Superman
   b. Daffy Duck
   c. the president

4. **In this story, a screen is:**
   a. what movies and TV are shown on
   b. something that keeps the bugs out
   c. a loud noise

5. **Mel Blanc probably:**
   a. plays the piano
   b. doesn't like insects
   c. liked his job

Page 42

A Trip Around the World

In 1965, **Robin Graham** began his trip around the world. He was going to travel in a sailboat called the **Dove**. Robin was only sixteen years old.

Robin's father had helped him get ready for the trip. His father had also taught him to sail. But now Robin was all alone. Sometimes the trip seemed easy. The sun was shining. There was just enough wind to sail the boat. But sometimes there were bad storms. It rained for hours. Big waves splashed on the boat. During one big storm, part of the boat broke. Robin fell into the ocean and almost drowned. He pulled himself back onto the boat just in time.

In 1971, Robin finished his trip. He had sailed over 30,000 miles. He had met interesting people all over the world. He had seen strange fish, whales and seals. It had been a great adventure.

1. **The main idea of this story is:**
   a. a big storm
   b. sailing around the world
   c. walking around the world

2. **Robin made the whole trip:**
   a. by himself
   b. with his father
   c. with some friends

3. **What was the name of Robin's boat?**
   a. the Whale
   b. the Sea
   c. the Dove

4. **Just in time means:**
   a. before it is too late
   b. what time it is
   c. trying to be on time

5. **One reason it took Robin five years to make his trip probably was:**
   a. He stopped in many different places.
   b. He was lazy.
   c. He didn't like sailing.

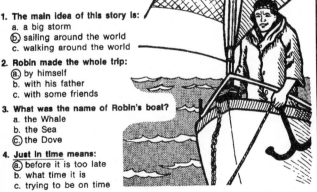

Page 43

Up, Up and Away!

On August 28, 1978, a balloon landed in a wheat field in **France**. When three men got out of the balloon's basket, people began cheering. The three men had just crossed the ocean in a balloon. They had traveled 3,100 miles. No one else had ever done this. The men's names were **Ben Abruzzo**, **Max Anderson** and **Larry Newman**.

The balloon was as high as a tall building. The men took along a boat in case something went wrong. Sometimes it got very cold high up in the air. They wore long underwear and had a little heater to keep warm. Once ice formed on the balloon. The big balloon began to go down. It looked like they might need the boat. But the sun melted the ice. The balloon rose up again. After five days the men finally reached land.

1. **The main idea of this story is:**
   a. Three men cross the ocean in a balloon.
   b. Three men cross the ocean in an airplane.
   c. One man takes a balloon around the world.

2. **The three men were the first people to:**
   a. cross the ocean in a balloon
   b. sail around the world
   c. take a balloon up in the air

3. **How many miles did the balloon travel?**
   a. 310 miles
   b. 3,000 miles
   c. 3,100 miles

4. **In this story in case means:**
   a. something you put things in
   b. if something should happen
   c. another way to travel

5. **If the ice had not melted, the balloon might have:**
   a. become very light
   b. sunk into the ocean
   c. changed colors

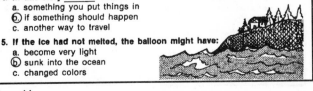

Page 44

FS-32045 Reading

Answer Key

Name _____ Date _____

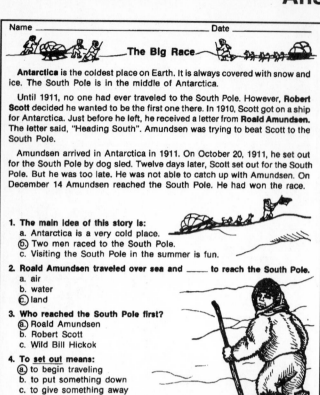

The Big Race

Antarctica is the coldest place on Earth. It is always covered with snow and ice. The South Pole is in the middle of Antarctica.

Until 1911, no one had ever traveled to the South Pole. However, **Robert Scott** decided he wanted to be the first one there. In 1910, Scott got on a ship for Antarctica. Just before he left, he received a letter from **Roald Amundsen**. The letter said, "Heading South". Amundsen was trying to beat Scott to the South Pole.

Amundsen arrived in Antarctica in 1911. On October 20, 1911, he set out for the South Pole by dog sled. Twelve days later, Scott set out for the South Pole. But he was too late. He was not able to catch up with Amundsen. On December 14 Amundsen reached the South Pole. He had won the race.

1. The main idea of this story is:
   a. Antarctica is a very cold place.
   b. Two men raced to the South Pole.
   c. Visiting the South Pole in the summer is fun.

2. Roald Amundsen traveled over sea and _____ to reach the South Pole.
   a. air
   b. water
   c. land

3. Who reached the South Pole first?
   a. Roald Amundsen
   b. Robert Scott
   c. Wild Bill Hickok

4. To set out means:
   a. to begin traveling
   b. to put something down
   c. to give something away

5. One animal that might live at the South Pole is a:
   a. seal
   b. camel
   c. lizard

Page 45

Name _____ Date _____

The Man Who Loves Adventure

Naomi Uemura is a hero in Japan. But he is almost never there. Naomi loves travel and adventure. His biggest adventure so far has been his trip to the North Pole.

In 1978 Naomi began his trip by land to the North Pole. He traveled by dog sled. Naomi wore bearskin pants, fur mittens and heavy boots. There were many big snowstorms along the way. Sometimes the trail was blocked by small hills of ice. Then Naomi had to cut through the ice.

Once a polar bear visited his camp. Naomi pretended he was sleeping. The bear ate most of Naomi's food and ripped his tent. An airplane dropped more food for Naomi. Then, one of his dogs had puppies. Naomi sent the mother and puppies back and got more dogs. After 54 days Naomi reached the North Pole. He was the first man to make the trip alone.

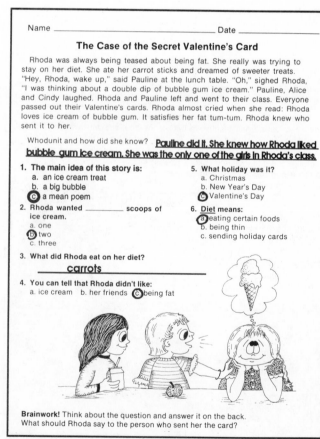

1. The main idea of this story is:
   a. A man travels to the North Pole alone.
   b. A polar bear eats all the food.
   c. A dog had puppies.

2. On his trip, Naomi wore:
   a. a bathing suit
   b. warm clothing
   c. light clothing

3. What is the name of Naomi's country?
   a. United States
   b. Japan
   c. England

4. The word **ripped** means:
   a. hurt
   b. made
   c. tore into pieces

5. It is probably very _____ at the North Pole.
   a. cold
   b. warm
   c. dry

Page 46

Name _____

Clara Barton was a great American woman who devoted her life to helping others. She founded the American Red Cross, a group which still helps millions of people.

During the Civil War she carried supplies to soldiers and nursed the wounded men. She was called the Angel of the Battlefield. At first the American government didn't help her, but later they realized how important she was.

She realized that the Red Cross could help people other than soldiers. Many of our people have been helped in time of emergency by the Red Cross. People need help during a disaster such as a flood.

Clara Barton took part in many kinds of **charitable** (volunteer) work. She wrote books and did patriotic work too.

1. The best title for this article is:
   a. Mrs. Clara Barton
   b. A Helpful Citizen
   c. Clara Barton, a Great American
   d. Helping Others

2. During the Civil War, Clara Barton was:
   a. an American officer
   b. a soldier
   c. a nurse
   d. a housewife

3. We will always remember that she began the:
   a. Red Cross
   b. nursing homes
   c. Civil War
   d. patriotic clubs

4. At first the American government:
   a. encouraged her
   b. wouldn't let her help
   c. paid her
   d. didn't realize her value

5. The word **volunteer** means:
   a. a mother
   b. a good person
   c. someone who helps without pay
   d. a nurse

6. Another happening much like the disaster mentioned in the story is:
   a. an earthquake
   b. rain
   c. a vacation
   d. a holiday

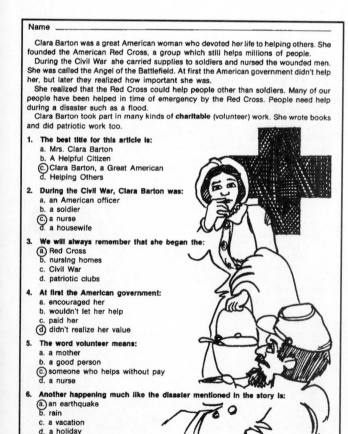

Page 47

Name _____ Date _____

The Case of the Secret Valentine's Card

Rhoda was always being teased about being fat. She really was trying to stay on her diet. She ate her carrot sticks and dreamed of sweeter treats. "Hey, Rhoda, wake up," said Pauline at the lunch table. "Oh," sighed Rhoda, "I was thinking about a double dip of bubble gum ice cream." Pauline, Alice and Cindy laughed. Rhoda and Pauline left and went to their class. Everyone passed out their Valentine's cards. Rhoda almost cried when she read: Rhoda loves ice cream of bubble gum. It satisfies her fat tum-tum. Rhoda knew who sent it to her.

Whodunit and how did she know? _Pauline did it. She knew how Rhoda liked bubble gum ice cream. She was the only one of the girls in Rhoda's class._

1. The main idea of this story is:
   a. an ice cream treat
   b. a big bubble
   c. a mean poem

2. Rhoda wanted _____ scoops of ice cream.
   a. one
   b. two
   c. three

3. What did Rhoda eat on her diet? _carrots_

4. You can tell that Rhoda didn't like:
   a. ice cream   b. her friends   **c.** being fat

5. What holiday was it?
   a. Christmas
   b. New Year's Day
   c. Valentine's Day

6. **Diet** means:
   a. eating certain foods
   b. being thin
   c. sending holiday cards

Brainwork! Think about the question and answer it on the back. What should Rhoda say to the person who sent her the card?

Page 48

Answer Key

Jesse James (1847-1882) was a bandit. He robbed banks and trains in Missouri and nearby states.

He joined forces with his brother and several other men. The **band** of eight men tried to rob a bank at Northfield, Minnesota in 1876. Citizens fought them off, killing three and capturing three others. Only Jesse and his brother Frank escaped. During that year Jesse moved to St. Joseph, Missouri, where he posed as a cattle buyer and called himself Tom Howard. In the end he was shot by Robert Ford, a traitor from his own band.

1. **This story was written to:**
   a. tell about a living person
   (b) give a brief picture of a man who lived years ago
   c. entertain a reader
   d. tell about an outstanding leader

2. **Jesse once posed as:**
   (a) a cattle buyer
   b. a cattle thief
   c. a bank robber
   d. a train robber

3. **Tom Howard was:**
   a. a governor who offered a reward for Jesse
   b. the brother of Jesse
   (c) a name Jesse used
   d. a man who shot Jesse

4. **During the robbery at Northfield, the James Brothers:**
   a. were shot
   b. were captured
   (c) managed to escape
   d. were wounded

5. **The word "band," as used in this story, means:**
   a. a musical group
   b. a strip of rubber
   (c) a group of men
   d. none of these

6. **We can assume Jesse died:**
   a. in prison in 1882
   b. during a robbery
   (c) from a shot fired by one of his own men in 1882
   d. of old age

JAIL

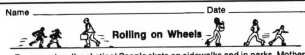

Rolling on Wheels

Everyone is roller skating! People skate on sidewalks and in parks. Mothers skate to the market and children skate to school. One man even skates 20 miles to work every day. Some people like to listen to music when they skate. They **wear** radios that fit over their ears. Other people like to wear fancy clothes when they skate.

People learn to dance or do tricks on skates. Some people can leap over lines of trash cans. Other people can skate backwards. **Champion** skaters often enter racing or dancing contests.

There are many different kinds of skates. The older skates had wood or metal wheels. Today most skates have big **rubber** wheels. If you feel tired, you can even buy skates with motors. Then, just stand up and let the skates roll you home!

1. **The main idea of this story is:**
   (a) People use skates in many different ways.
   b. Skating backwards is fun.
   c. People don't enjoy skating.

2. **Skaters can enter:**
   a. cooking contests
   b. beauty contests
   (c) skating contests

3. **Today most skate wheels are made of:**
   a. wood
   (b) rubber
   c. metal

4. **Champion skaters are:**
   a. losers
   b. scared
   (c) winners

5. **If you go too fast on skates you may:**
   a. start flying
   (b) fall down
   c. climb up a tree

Jumps and Bumps

It's the day of the big motorcycle race. The racers are dressed in **leather** pants, **jackets**, boots and gloves. They all wear safety **helmets**.

It will be a hard race. The race will be held on a dirt track. The track has two jumps and some big mud puddles.

What a lot of noise! The engines have started up. The racers are lined up at the starting line. The race begins! The track has a lot of bumps in it. One man's motorcycle turns over but he is all right. There's the first jump. A racer takes the jump. His cycle lifts off the ground and then lands on its back wheel.

Another motorcycle gets stuck in the mud and its wheels begin to spin. Some racers drop out of the race. The winner is covered with mud and dust. But he is very happy.

1. **The main idea of this story is:**
   a. Racers keep their clothes very clean.
   (b) Motorcycle racing is an exciting sport.
   c. Motorcycle racers go to school.

2. **Motorcycle engines are:**
   a. very quiet
   b. very small
   (c) very noisy

3. **All motorcycle racers wear:**
   (a) safety helmets
   b. white shoes
   c. baseball caps

4. **The word jacket means:**
   a. shirt
   b. tie
   (c) short coat

5. **Motorcycle racers must be careful:**
   a. not to make too much noise
   (b) not to turn over their cycles
   c. to stay clean

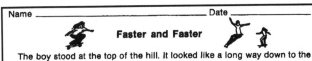

Faster and Faster

The boy stood at the top of the hill. It looked like a long way down to the bottom. He put on his **helmet, knee** pads and **elbow** pads. He placed one foot on his skateboard and pushed off with the other foot. Suddenly, he saw some bumps in the middle of the road. He leaned to the right and the skateboard moved to the right. He just missed the bumps. He began going faster and faster. Soon he was going over 30 miles an hour. He reached the bottom. He turned his board to the side and stopped.

Skateboards have four small wheels. Boards are made of **plastic**, metal or wood. Good skateboard riders can do many tricks. They skate in special parks, safe streets or on sidewalks. Some skateboard riders even skate up the walls of empty swimming pools!

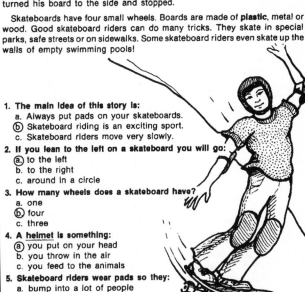

1. **The main idea of this story is:**
   a. Always put pads on your skateboards.
   (b) Skateboard riding is an exciting sport.
   c. Skateboard riders move very slowly.

2. **If you lean to the left on a skateboard you will go:**
   (a) to the left
   b. to the right
   c. around in a circle

3. **How many wheels does a skateboard have?**
   a. one
   (b) four
   c. three

4. **A helmet is something:**
   (a) you put on your head
   b. you throw in the air
   c. you feed to the animals

5. **Skateboard riders wear pads so they:**
   a. bump into a lot of people
   (b) won't hurt themselves when they fall
   c. can jump high in the air

FS-32045 Reading

Answer Key

Name _____ Date _____

Welcome to the Wild West

This is just like the Wild West. Today is the opening of the rodeo. Cowboys and cowgirls have come from all over to enter the contests. During the year they work on ranches. They rope cattle and ride horses all day. Once a year they can show off these **skills** at the rodeo.

The first contest is **bronc** riding. A bronc is a wild horse. One horse is called Fireball. He looks very mean. The cowboy gets on Fireball and tries to hang on. The horse kicks his legs in the air. He jumps up and down. But the cowboy stays on Fireball for ten seconds. He wins the contest.

Now it's time for the barrel race. Sue Green rides her horse around three barrels. She doesn't knock down any barrels. Some of the other cowgirls do knock down barrels. Sue is the winner.

It has been an exciting day. Tomorrow the cowboys and cowgirls will be headed back to their ranches.

1. **The main idea of this story is:**
   a. A rodeo is made up of different contests. *(a circled)*
   b. Only cowboys can enter rodeos.
   c. There are lions and tigers at rodeos.

2. **Cowgirls and cowboys learn to rope and ride:**
   a. at the beach
   b. on ranches *(circled)*
   c. in the jungle

3. **How many barrels are there in a barrel race?**
   a. three *(circled)*
   b. two
   c. four

4. **A bronc is:**
   a. a bull
   b. a wild horse *(circled)*
   c. a wild cow

5. **A cowboy or cowgirl should be:**
   a. very funny
   b. a good rider *(circled)*
   c. a fast runner

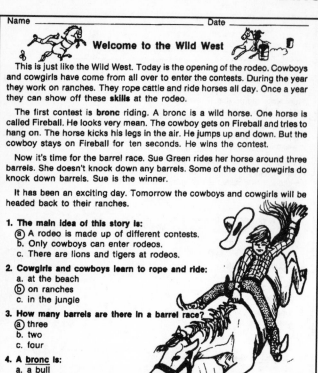

Page 53

Name _____ Date _____

A Day at the Circus

The band begins to play. It's time for the circus! First there is a big parade around the ring. Women in beautiful costumes ride on elephants. Next, clown drives a little car around the ring. He stops the car and out come 2 clowns!

The parade ends and the show begins. First, the horseback rider leaps into the air and lands on her horse. Then, the animal trainer comes out. He walks into a cage filled with lions and tigers. The lions and tigers growl and show their teeth. But the animal trainer is not afraid. He waves a small stick in the air. The animals jump onto little **stools**.

Finally, a man walks across the high wire. He is very high up in the air. The wire begins to shake. It looks like he will fall. He walks to the end of the wire and jumps safely onto the **platform**. Everyone claps their hands. What a wonderful show!

1. **The main idea of this story is:**
   a. going to the circus *(circled)*
   b. going to the zoo
   c. watching a big parade

2. **The circus has:**
   a. many different things to see *(circled)*
   b. no animals in the show
   c. airplanes

3. **Who works with the lions and tigers?**
   a. the clowns
   b. the animal trainer *(circled)*
   c. the man on the high wire

4. **The word platform means:**
   a. a big table
   b. the end of a wire
   c. a flat stage above the ground *(circled)*

5. **Animal trainers probably:**
   a. like working with animals *(circled)*
   b. are afraid of animals
   c. want to become clowns

Page 54

Name _____ Date _____

A Town for Little People

Madurodam in **Holland** looks like many other towns. It has houses, roads, parks and an airport. The street lights turn on at night. Cars and buses move along the highways. There is a big traffic jam downtown. In the park, the merry-go-round turns round and round. But there is something very different about this city. Many of the buildings are shorter than a person's leg. The street lights are only as tall as pencils standing on end. And the people are three inches tall.

Of course the people are only little dolls. Everything in Madurodam is much smaller than in real life. The little buildings are **models** of real buildings in Holland. Since Madurodam was first built, over 15 million people have visited it. Parents enjoy the tiny city as much as their children.

1. **The main idea of this story is:**
   a. a town for giants
   b. people are three inches tall
   c. a town where everything is little *(circled)*

2. **Madurodam is different than other cities in:**
   a. size *(circled)*
   b. color
   c. number of buildings

3. **In what country is Madurodam?**
   a. Holland *(circled)*
   b. England
   c. the United States

4. **The word model means:**
   a. a new kind of food
   b. a small copy of something *(circled)*
   c. a new way to make things

5. **A car in Madurodam might be the size of:**
   a. a desk
   b. a horse
   c. an apple *(circled)*

Page 55

Name _____ Date _____

A Statue for Freedom

The **Statue of Liberty** stands in New York Harbor. It is known all over the world. It is a statue of a beautiful woman. She wears a crown on her head. But she is not a queen. In one hand she holds a book of law. In the other hand she holds a light. At night the light can be seen from far away.

France gave the statue to the United States in 1884. It is one of the largest statues ever made. The statue is 151 feet tall. It weighs 450,000 pounds. There is a staircase leading to the top of its crown. From the top, visitors can see the harbor and New York City. The Statue of Liberty stands for freedom. It is the first thing many people see when they enter the United States. It means they have come to a free country.

1. **The main idea of this story is:**
   a. boats in the harbor
   b. a big boat
   c. facts about a famous statue *(circled)*

2. **The Statue of Liberty is:**
   a. very heavy *(circled)*
   b. in England
   c. in the middle of the desert

3. **Who gave the Statue of Liberty to the United States?**
   a. Soviet Union
   b. France *(circled)*
   c. England

4. **The word liberty means:**
   a. to be free *(circled)*
   b. to buy something
   c. to go to the movies

5. **The Statue of Liberty is probably made of:**
   a. paper
   b. feathers
   c. metal *(circled)*

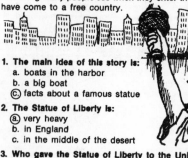

Page 56

118

Answer Key

The Magic Kingdom

The Jones family was going to **Disneyland**. Sara Jones was very excited. "I hope I see Mickey Mouse and Donald Duck," she said.

When they arrived, Sara thought Disneyland looked like a magic **kingdom**. There was a beautiful castle in the middle of the park. And there were her friends, Mickey and Donald, waving at her.

First Sara went on the Jungle Boat Ride. She saw elephants, lions and zebras. Then Sara went on the Submarine Ride. It went under the water. A big sea **monster** was swimming in the water. The monster looked like it was smiling.

There were so many things to do. There were train rides and a merry-go-round. One exciting ride was the **Matterhorn**. Sara got into a little car on tracks. It went up and down the mountain very fast. At night, fireworks went off in the park. It was the end of a wonderful day.

1. **The main idea of this story is:**
   a. There are monsters in Disneyland.
   b. Mickey Mouse lives in Disneyland.
   c.) There are many things to do in Disneyland.

2. **The sea monster seemed:**
   a.) friendly
   b. angry
   c. scary

3. **The first ride Sara rode was:**
   a. the Submarine Ride
   b.) the Jungle Boat Ride
   c. the Spaceship Ride

4. **A kingdom is:**
   a. a big zoo
   b. a house filled with people
   c.) a country ruled by a king

5. **To see all of Disneyland, it would probably take:**
   a. a half hour
   b. one year
   c.) all day

The President's House

Imagine you were president of the United States. You would meet important people from all over the world. Sometimes you would travel to different cities and talk to the American people. You would even be able to live in the White House.

The White House is painted all white on the outside. It was first built in 1800. But the first building burned down. The White House was rebuilt in 1817. Since then, all the presidents have lived there. Each one has changed the White House a little. Today, the White House has 132 rooms. Some of the rooms are named after colors. There is a Red Room, a Blue Room and a Green Room. The dining room can seat 140 people. Imagine what your mother would say if you brought 140 people home for dinner!

1. **The main idea of this story is:**
   a. how to become a president
   b.) about the White House
   c. building the White House

2. **The White House is:**
   a. less than 50 years old
   b.) more than 150 years old
   c. 10 years old

3. **Some of the rooms are named after:**
   a.) colors
   b. animals
   c. people

4. **In this story the word seat means:**
   a. a big pillow to sit on
   b.) how many people can sit in a room
   c. sitting down at the same time

5. **Another person who might live in the White House is:**
   a. a rock star
   b.) the President's wife
   c. the Queen of England

A Floating City

In **Venice, Italy**, children don't ride buses to school. They ride motor boats. Venice is a city made up of 120 small islands. There are no roads in the city. But there are waterways called **canals**. People use boats instead of cars or buses. Some people ride in long rowboats called **gondolas**. There are over 150 canals in the city. If people want to take a walk, they use the walkways along the canals. There are also 400 bridges which cross over the canals.

Venice is a very beautiful city. It has many old buildings. But it is not always a safe place to live. Sometimes when it rains, the houses get filled with water. And for a long time Venice was sinking a little every year. People were afraid that one day Venice would sink into the ocean. But the problem was solved and the city was saved.

1. **The main idea of this story is:**
   a. a safe place to live
   b.) a city made up of small islands
   c. a city with many roads

2. **People who live in Venice worry about:**
   a. too little water
   b. snowstorms
   c.) too much rain

3. **How do people travel in Venice?**
   a. in trucks
   b.) in boats
   c. in cars

4. **The word canal means:**
   a.) waterway
   b. river
   c. street

5. **Venice is probably very:**
   a. new
   b. ugly
   c.) old

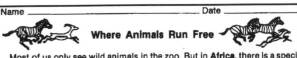

Where Animals Run Free

Most of us only see wild animals in the zoo. But in **Africa**, there is a special park just for wild animals. The park is called **Serengeti**. In Serengeti zebras, buffalos, lions and elephants run free. There are also giraffes, wild dogs and monkeys in the park.

The animals like Serengeti because there is a lot of good grass to eat. The park also has many streams and lakes. Elephants fill their trunks with water from the streams and take baths. Monkeys play games and dig for bugs with sticks. Tall giraffes eat leaves from the treetops. Thousands of zebras gather in one place to eat grass.

There are also dangers in Serengeti. Lions hunt the zebras and buffalos. Large snakes creep through the grass. In Serengeti, each day is filled with adventure.

1. **The main idea of this story is:**
   a. Serengeti is a big zoo.
   b.) There are no cages in Serengeti.
   c. Only people live in Serengeti.

2. **In the United States, most wild animals live:**
   a. in houses
   b. in parks
   c.) in zoos

3. **The animals like Serengeti because there is:**
   a.) a lot of grass to eat
   b. popcorn and soda
   c. television

4. **If there are dangers, then a place is:**
   a. safe
   b. fun
   c.) not safe

5. **If Serengeti was a desert, it would probably:**
   a. have a lot of water
   b. be very cold
   c.) not have many animals

© Frank Schaffer Publications, Inc.

Answer Key

Name _____ Date _____

Boiling Water

In **Yellowstone Park**, creeks are filled with hot, bubbling water. A river in this park is cold on top and hot on the bottom. And there are holes in the ground that blow out steam. The steam holes are called **geysers**. The steam and heat comes from inside the earth. There are over 10,000 geysers and hot springs in Yellowstone.

The best known geyser is **Old Faithful**. Every 65 minutes it sprays out steam and hot water. It uses 10,000 gallons of water in four minutes. Sometimes the water spray is over 100 feet tall.

Geysers are very interesting, but they can also be very tricky. Once a man tried to wash his clothes in a geyser. He put his clothes and soap in it. Just then the geyser blew up. The man's clothes went flying in the air.

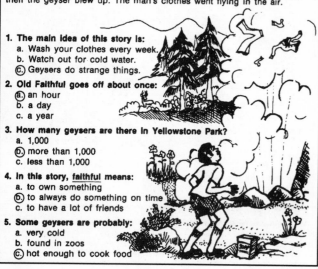

1. **The main idea of this story is:**
   a. Wash your clothes every week.
   b. Watch out for cold water.
   c. Geysers do strange things.

2. **Old Faithful goes off about once:**
   a. an hour
   b. a day
   c. a year

3. **How many geysers are there in Yellowstone Park?**
   a. 1,000
   b. more than 1,000
   c. less than 1,000

4. **In this story, faithful means:**
   a. to own something
   b. to always do something on time
   c. to have a lot of friends

5. **Some geysers are probably:**
   a. very cold
   b. found in zoos
   c. hot enough to cook food

Page 61

Name _____ Date _____

Rock Trees

Once there were tall trees standing in the **Petrified** Forest. The forest also had bushes, flowers and streams. But that was millions of years ago. Today the grass is gone and the land has become a desert. The trees have fallen down and lie on the ground. They look soft. But they are hard enough to break a saw. They can only be cut with special tools. The trees have turned to stone.

Many years ago a big flood knocked down many of the trees. They were buried in the mud. Then water with metal in it dripped into the trees. Slowly the trees turned to stone. The wind and rain uncovered them after thousands of years. Today there are only wood chips, tree stumps and logs in the forest. Some of the logs are 100 feet long. More logs may still be buried deep in the ground.

1. **The main idea of this story is:**
   a. Trees have turned to stone.
   b. There are many streams in the Petrified Forest.
   c. The trees in the Petrified Forest are easy to cut.

2. **Some of the logs in the forest are very:**
   a. soft
   b. good to eat
   c. long

3. **Today the Petrified Forest is a:**
   a. city
   b. desert
   c. farm

4. **A petrified tree is made of:**
   a. wood
   b. food
   c. stone

5. **From this story you can tell the trees are:**
   a. dead
   b. still growing
   c. green

Page 62

Name _____ Date _____

Strange Stones

The **Carlsbad Caverns** are large caves deep under the ground. One of the caves is the largest in the world. It is big enough to cover fourteen football fields. The Carlsbad Caverns are very old. Animals lived in the caves over 200 **million** years ago. Today, only bats live there. At one time there were over eight million bats in the caves.

Every year many people visit the Carlsbad Caverns. In the caves there are big lights so people can see the **limestone** rocks. Some of the rocks look like animals or people. One rock is called Whale's Mouth. Another rock is called Three Little Monkeys. There is even a rock that looks like Santa Claus. The rocks were formed by dripping water. Some rocks hang from the ceiling. Other rocks rise up from the floor.

At the end of the walk, visitors eat in a lunchroom 754 feet under the ground.

1. **The main idea of this story is:**
   a. Some caves are very small.
   b. Carlsbad Caverns has interesting rocks.
   c. Carlsbad Caverns is a very dark place.

2. **Some of the caves in the Carlsbad Caverns are:**
   a. very light
   b. filled with snakes
   c. very large

3. **Animals lived in the caves over:**
   a. 200 million years ago
   b. 200 years ago
   c. 50 million years ago

4. **Limestone is a:**
   a. stone fruit
   b. kind of rock
   c. cold drink

5. **Since the caves are underground, you can guess that:**
   a. A lot of plants grow there.
   b. They are very dark.
   c. Birds fly around.

Page 63

Name _____

If you're thinking about ordering an extra paper to read during the evening, let me offer you a word of warning: Beware of Bruce! Bruce wanted to win a trip to camp, so I was more than glad to help him out by taking the newspaper.

The first night, Bruce whizzed by on his bike and tossed the paper over my fence. What aim! It landed in the garbage and I didn't find it for two days, yellowed and fading. The next day, our dog, Beetle, found the paper first and chewed it to shreds trying to get the rubber band off. On the third day, I got the paper all in one piece—right through the front window!

I hope Bruce goes to camp and gives up his paper route!

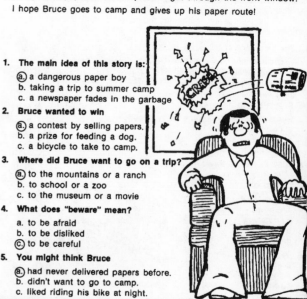

1. **The main idea of this story is:**
   a. a dangerous paper boy
   b. taking a trip to summer camp
   c. a newspaper fades in the garbage

2. **Bruce wanted to win**
   a. a contest by selling papers.
   b. a prize for feeding a dog.
   c. a bicycle to take to camp.

3. **Where did Bruce want to go on a trip?**
   a. to the mountains or a ranch
   b. to school or a zoo
   c. to the museum or a movie

4. **What does "beware" mean?**
   a. to be afraid
   b. to be disliked
   c. to be careful

5. **You might think Bruce**
   a. had never delivered papers before.
   b. didn't want to go to camp.
   c. liked riding his bike at night.

Page 64

120

FS-32045 Readin

Answer Key

Name _____

"Yesterday afternoon I brought a nice wood box down from the attic, and now it's gone. Quite a few things have been disappearing from this living room lately. Do you know what's happened, Davy?"

"I think the ghost that lives upstairs came down and took it back," Davy told his mother. "He likes certain things up there to make him feel at home. Maybe we should try to find an old table and chair to make him more comfortable when he's not out haunting houses. Come to think of it, I'll bet that ghost would like to have a television set, too. If we keep him happy, I just know that ghost will never bother you, Mom."

BOY, I COULD REALLY USE A T.V. SET!

The main idea of this story is:

a. a ghost comes to live with Davy
b. a ghost that likes to feel at home ✓
c. a story of a haunted house

Mother felt there was something

a. alive in the living room.
b. terrible happening.
c. mysterious going on. ✓

Where did the ghost live?

a. in a haunted house
b. in the attic ✓
c. in Davy's room

Another word for "disappearing" would be:

a. happening
b. vanishing ✓
c. describing

You might think that the ghost was:

a. moving out of the house
b. Davy himself ✓
c. a thief

Page 65

Name _____

I have a younger brother who could easily win the "Pest Of The Year Award". When Mark was four years old, he was just your average, run-of-the-mill pest. Today, three years later, he has developed into a first-class trouble maker. One evening, I found Mark outside collecting insects in a jar. "What are you doing, Mark?"

"I'm catching these for you to add to your bug collection, Wendy."

"Isn't that thoughtful," I said to myself. But I should have known better. A few hours later, I walked into my room and there sitting in my bookcase were fifteen grasshoppers, grinning from ear to ear. They were so full from having gulped down my entire bug collection, all they could do was hiccup. No more favors, please!

1. **The main idea of this story is:**

   a. a pest "bugs" his sister ✓
   b. collecting insects at night in the garden
   c. the grasshopper's dinner feast

2. **Bug collecting can be a favorite hobby or a**

   a. waste of time.
   b. part of science. ✓
   c. dinner party.

3. **How old is Mark in the story?**

   a. 4 years old
   b. 7 years old ✓
   c. you can't tell

4. **What is another good word for "gulped"?**

   a. choked
   b. swallowed ✓
   c. tasted

5. **The jar Mark used probably**

   a. wasn't very large.
   b. didn't have a lid on it. ✓
   c. had peanut butter in it.

Page 66

Name _____

"Uh-oh, I think my hamster escaped! I've got to find him."

"Joey, I told you not to bring that animal in here! Pets aren't allowed in grocery stores," mother scolded him.

"I see his tail," Joey shouted, shoving his hand into a stack of paper towels. But the hamster scampered away and towels rolled everywhere. "I see two ears sticking up between those cans. I'll get him now," Joey yelled climbing up on a shelf. Down clattered eighteen cans of carrots, ten cans of beets and eight cans of green beans.

Just then the store owner dashed over to Joey's mother. "From now on, I don't think I'll allow children in my store. They are more dangerous than animals!"

1. **The main idea of this story is:**

   a. children can be dangerous too ✓
   b. paper towels rolling off shelves
   c. a hamster hides from mother

2. **Joey knocked over**

   a. cans of fruit.
   b. cans of vegetables. ✓
   c. cans of soup.

3. **What was Joey trying to do?**

   a. get a roll of paper towels
   b. capture his hamster ✓
   c. ruin the store

4. **Paper towels come on a "roll". Another kind of "role" is**

   a. a part in a play. ✓
   b. a coffee-cake.
   c. a bouncing ball.

5. **From the story you cannot tell if**

   a. Joey caught the hamster. ✓
   b. towels spilled everywhere.
   c. mother was angry at Joey.

Page 67

Name _____

For two years I worked very hard learning to be a good speller, harder than you can imagine! I studied twenty new words every week for about two hours, and most of the time I got "A"s on my tests. I didn't think there was a single word I couldn't spell by sounding out the letters and knowing a few other secrets, like "i before e except after c".

Yesterday we had a surprise test. When I saw my paper today, I was as mad as a bumblebee! I spelled "photograph"—"fotograf", "knife"—"nife" and "cough"—"cof". This doesn't make any sense to me at all. The person who wrote the dictionary should come to school with me and learn how to spell!

SURE I CAN SPELL "EMPTY"! IT'S SPELLED "M, T"!

1. **The main idea of this story is:**

   a. students studying for a spelling test
   b. spelling doesn't make any sense ✓
   c. rewriting a dictionary

2. **Some letters in a word**

   a. are not in the alphabet.
   b. have three different sounds.
   c. make no sound or different sounds. ✓

3. **One thing the story doesn't tell is:**

   a. how to spell photograph
   b. how many words were studied
   c. how everyone else did on the test ✓

4. **"To make sense" means to "be clear". Another kind of sense is:**

   a. the sense of taste ✓
   b. the sense of action
   c. the sense of direction

5. **You can guess that the person in the story**

   a. did not have a good memory.
   b. was confused by silent letters and odd spelling. ✓
   c. wanted to try again and take another test.

Page 68

Answer Key

Name _____

As I ran upstairs to bed, I heard Mom say, "Hang your uniform in the closet." It was the night before the big game and I really wanted to win. I was very tired, so I dropped my clothes over a chair and climbed quickly into bed. I was soon asleep.

In the morning I dressed quickly. One sock was missing. Who could have taken my sock? I was so sure I had put everything on the chair. I looked everywhere. I had to play the big game with only one team sock. We lost the game.

When I got home I saw a **touch** of blue and gold in Skipper's box. Skipper had taken my sock. I thought about it for a while. Skipper couldn't reach the clothes on my chair. How did my dog get my sock?

1. **The most interesting title for this story is:**
   a. Why You Should Hang Up Your Clothes
   b. Be Prepared
   c. The Big Game
   (d.) The Mystery of the Missing Sock

2. **The story took place:**
   a. before a big game
   b. in the morning
   c. at night
   (d.) at several times

3. **The person in the story didn't hang up his clothes because:**
   a. he was in a hurry to leave
   (b.) he was tired
   c. he was too excited
   d. he didn't know how

4. **The reason his team lost the game was:**
   a. he didn't have a sock
   b. he couldn't play without his whole uniform
   c. the other team was really great
   (d.) the story doesn't say

5. **The word "touch," in the story means:**
   a. put one's finger on
   b. tap lightly
   (c.) a small amount
   d. a color

6. **Most likely the dog got the sock because:**
   a. he pulled it off the chair
   b. someone gave it to him
   (c.) it had fallen on the floor
   d. a larger dog found it first

Page 69

Name _____

Although there seem to be **countless** stars in the sky, there are even more different kinds of insects. Scientists have found more than 800,000 kinds of insects, but authorities believe there may be as many as 4,000,000 species.

Insects live nearly everywhere they can find food. It is hard to find food in the oceans, therefore very few insects are found there.

The insect plays a most important part in our lives because he eats so much and in getting food, he aids man. The honey-bee is an example of helpfulness.

Other insects are harmful. They bite men and destroy millions of dollars in crops each year.

1. **The best title for this story is:**
   a. Hundreds of Insects
   (b.) Interesting Insects
   c. How Insects Help Us
   d. How Insects Hurt Us

2. **Scientists have identified more than:**
   a. 4 million species of insects
   b. several species of insects
   (c.) 800,000 kinds of insects
   d. only a few species

3. **Few insects live in the oceans because:**
   a. it is too wet there
   b. they can't fly underwater
   (c.) they find little food there
   d. they can't do much damage there

4. **Insects are:**
   a. helpful
   b. harmful
   c. large
   (d.) both A and B

5. **The word "countless" means:**
   a. less than we can count
   b. countable
   (c.) more than we can count
   d. not too many

6. **Since some insects are harmful:**
   a. insects should be killed
   (b.) harmful insects need to be destroyed or controlled as much as possible
   c. we should get more helpful insects
   d. we don't need any insects

Page 70

Name _____

A soapbox derby is a coasting race for small motorless racing cars. The race was named soapbox because sometimes the cars are made from wooden soapboxes.

The contestants are kids between the ages of 11 and 15. They build the racing cars. There are rules which govern the size and **weight** of the racer, how it is built and how much it can cost.

There are local races. The winners of these races then attend the All-American and International Soapbox Derby in Akron, Ohio. A college scholarship is offered to the winner of these final contests.

People from the United States, Canada, South America and Europe enter the Derby. Thousands of spectators view the race each year.

1. **The best title for this story is:**
   (a.) The Soapbox Derby
   b. Racing
   c. Children's Racing Derby
   d. A Racing Contest

2. **In the word "motorless," the suffix less means:**
   a. not as much
   b. little
   (c.) without a
   d. none of these

3. **You may spend _____ on the car you build:**
   a. any amount
   (b.) an amount stated in the rules
   c. a large amount
   d. a small amount

4. **The final races are held in:**
   a. Europe
   b. South America
   c. Canada
   (d.) none of these

5. **The word "weight" means:**
   (a.) heaviness
   b. amount
   c. pause a while
   d. stop

6. **We can assume that many people enjoy the Derbies because the article says:**
   a. everyone watches it
   b. millions of people watch it
   (c.) thousands of people see it
   d. only a few attend the Derby

Page 71

Name _____

The kangaroo rat is a tiny animal that jumps around like a kangaroo. The rat can leap on his powerful hind legs. His tail is about as long as his body.

He comes out at night to search for food. His eyes are large and he can see well in the dark.

Kangaroo rats have silky fur of yellow or brown on the upper parts of their bodies and white underparts. They can **stuff** food into fur-lined pouches on the outside of their cheeks. They do not need to drink water. They get water from inside themselves when their food combines with the oxygen they breathe.

These rats live in the deserts of the southwestern United States.

1. **The best title for this story is:**
   a. Small animals
   (b.) The Kangaroo Rat
   c. How Kangaroos Get Water
   d. How a Kangaroo Looks

2. **These rats are able to hunt for food at night because:**
   (a.) they can see well in the dark
   b. they know where to look
   c. they can smell food
   d. their eyes are too large

3. **These rats may be:**
   a. yellow and white
   b. brown and white
   (c.) either A and B
   d. brown and yellow

4. **If a kangaroo rat is about 15 inches including the tail, the tail is about:**
   a. 9 inches long
   b. 3 or 4 inches long
   (c.) about 7½ inches long
   d. there is no way to guess

5. **In this article, the word "stuff" means:**
   a. junk
   b. food
   (c.) place or put
   d. carry

6. **These rats probably survive well in desert areas because:**
   a. they have always lived there
   (b.) they don't need water
   c. it is nice and warm there
   d. people won't go there to hunt

Page 72

FS-32045 Reading

Answer Key

ome fish are able to **inflate** their bodies like balloons. The common name of such a
is "puffer fish" or "swell fish." Some common puffers live along the Atlantic coast,
le others live in tropical waters.

lost of the time the puffer looks like an ordinary fish with a large head and mouth that
ears to have teeth sticking out. When the fish is disturbed, it inflates its stomach with
After it is inflated, it floats belly upward on the surface of water until the danger has
ssed. It may blow itself to twice its normal size.

he name "puffer" may be confused with the word "puffin," which is actually an
d-looking bird that lives in the Arctic.

The two best titles for this story are:
a. (a) Inflatable Fish
b. Puffins
c. (c) Puffer Fish
d. Unusual Animals

Generally the fish inflates itself when:
a. it senses danger
b. it is happy
c. it is disturbed
d. (d) both A and C

When inflated, the fish is:
a. (a) two times as big as usual
b. smaller
c. three times larger than usual
d. many times larger than usual

The puffin is a:
a. fish
b. (b) a bird
c. another name for puffer
d. none of these

The word "swell" is a name that indicates a fish that:
a. is great
b. (b) can enlarge itself
c. is really super
d. is in rising swirls of water

From the way the word "inflate" is used in the story we can guess it means:
a. a balloon
b. (b) take in air
c. blows out
d. moves

Page 73

One of the greediest eaters and killers among sea animals is the shark. Sharks live in all
parts of the sea, but they seem to prefer warm areas. They may grow to be over 40 feet
long. Their bodies are covered with scales which give the skin a rough feeling much like
sandpaper. Although many sharks have rows of long, sharp teeth, others have broad, flat
teeth. Sharks can swim rapidly and may follow ships for days waiting for food to be
thrown overboard.

The largest shark, the whale shark, is harmless to man. It is often over 50 feet long but
feeds only on small sea animals and plants. This is the largest known fish. The whale,
which is larger, is not a fish. It is a mammal.

Sharks are used by man for making glue, fertilizer, cod-liver oil, leather and food.

1. **The best title for this story is:**
   a. The Many Uses of Sharks
   b. (b) Sharks
   c. Fish of Many Kinds
   d. The Largest Shark

2. **The largest known fish is:**
   a. a whale
   b. any shark
   c. (c) the whale shark
   d. the article doesn't say

3. **Sharks prefer areas that are:**
   a. (a) warm
   b. near people
   c. near boats
   d. near other fish

4. **The largest shark often:**
   a. eats people
   b. (b) is over 50 feet long
   c. eats large sea animals and plants
   d. swims faster than ships

5. **In this article, the word "parts" means:**
   a. pieces
   b. separates with a comb
   c. (c) sections
   d. bodies

6. **Sharks can be used for:**
   a. food
   b. leather
   c. fertilizer
   d. (d) all of these

Page 74

Small squirrels that can glide through the air are called flying squirrels. These squirrels
e in the forests of Asia, Europe and North America.

A fold of skin on each side of the squirrel's body connects the front and back legs.
en he stretches out his front and back legs, the skin makes gliding wings. As it glides
m tree to tree, the squirrel uses its broad flat tail to guide its flight. He can cover
m 50 to 100 feet in a leap, but generally covers about 50 to 60 feet.

These squirrels are only 8 to 12 inches long including their tails. They live in the
llows of trees and hunt for food only at night. Other squirrels hunt **by** day. They eat a
riety of things including berries, bird's eggs, insect, nuts, young birds or dead animals.

The main purpose of this story is to tell about:
a. squirrels
b. small animals
c. flying animals
d. (d) squirrels that seem to fly

The "wings" of the squirrel are formed by:
a. the legs
b. the arms
c. (c) folds of skin
d. all of these together

The "flight" is guided by:
a. the squirrel
b. the wind direction
c. (c) the animal's tail
d. the distance to travel

The flying squirrel usually leaps about:
a. 100 feet
b. over 75 feet
c. (c) 50 to 60 feet
d. under 15 feet

In the article, the word "by" means:
a. near
b. past
c. purchase
d. (d) during

These animals are probably considered different from other squirrels because:
a. they seem to fly
b. they hunt at night
c. they are 8 to 12 inches long
d. (d) both A and B

Page 75

Skin diving is another name for "free" diving. The diver goes underwater with no air
supply from which to breathe.

Skin divers explore the world beneath the surface of rivers, lakes or oceans. They may
take pictures, hunt fish or just study nature. This type of diving is usually done for
recreation.

Skin divers may also search for evidence in crimes or disasters, repair ships, or do
other important work under water. Since a skin diver can move around easily, he can do
jobs that would be difficult for a diver with a helmet and air hose.

Most skin divers wear face masks and rubber foot fins. They often use a snorkel, which
is a tube that allows them to breathe underwater.

1. **The best title for this story is:**
   a. Life Under Water
   b. Going for a Swim
   c. (c) The Art of Skin Diving
   d. Studying Fish

2. **The diver has no:**
   a. fins
   b. mask
   c. (c) air supply
   d. camera

3. **A detective might hire a skin diver:**
   a. (a) to find evidence
   b. to find a special fish
   c. to haul up a sunken ship
   d. to repair a boat

4. **It is easier for a skin diver to do some kinds of work than it would be for a diver with
   a helmet because:**
   a. he can stay underwater longer
   b. he takes up less space
   c. (c) he isn't connected to cords and can move easily
   d. he doesn't charge as much

5. **The word "recreation" means:**
   a. work
   b. (b) fun
   c. a park
   d. money

6. **One thing a skin diver must know is:**
   a. where a boat sank
   b. who will pay him
   c. how deep the water is
   d. (d) how to swim

Page 76

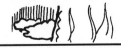

Answer Key

One day Jan was visiting her grandmother. Her grandmother had been cleaning drawers before Jan arrived and had left some of her favorite jewelry on the dresser. When Jan **saw** the jewelry, she decided to try on a bracelet.

Suddenly Grandmother called for her to come and eat some freshly baked cookies. She hurried downstairs and enjoyed the treat.

Later she went out to play with Pal, grandmother's dog. When she remembered the bracelet, she saw it was gone. She looked everywhere but she couldn't find it.

Jan was a very unhappy girl. She had taken something that wasn't her own. She knew she must tell Grandmother what happened. Grandmother said she would try to help.

1. **The best title for this story is:**
   a. A Happy Visit
   b. Grandmother's House
   c. Jan and Pal
   d. The Lost Bracelet ✓

2. **Jan made a mistake when:**
   a. she tried on the bracelet without permission ✓
   b. she went outside
   c. she played with the dog
   d. she ate too many cookies

3. **Jan was probably most unhappy because:**
   a. she had taken something that didn't belong to her ✓
   b. she knew Grandmother would be angry
   c. she lost the bracelet
   d. the dog had taken the bracelet

4. **She knew the best thing she could do now is:**
   a. tell the truth and ask for help ✓
   b. hunt some more
   c. buy a new bracelet
   d. cry

5. **In this story, the word "saw" means:**
   a. take the cover off
   b. see it through the grass
   c. found ✓
   d. look for it

6. **The best rule to follow is:**
   a. put back things you take
   b. get permission before borrowing things ✓
   c. don't lose things
   d. don't tell anyone if you lose something

Page 77

Ohio has changed from a farm state to a state famous for big, busy cities. It has an important steel center and factories which make glass and automobile pa[rts]. Great quantities of coal are **shipped** from Toledo, and Akron is the rubber city of [the] nation. Cincinnati makes soap, playing cards and machinery. The soil is rich and wh[ere] oats, corn, soybeans and tobacco are grown in Ohio. Eight U.S. presidents came from Ohio.

Ohio is called the "Buckeye State" because of the Buckeye leaves on many trees. It w[as] named after the Ohio River. Ohio means "beautiful river."

1. **The best title for this story is:**
   a. An Important State
   b. Ohio, An Important State ✓
   c. A State of Large Cities
   b. "Beautiful River"

2. **After reading the article we know that:**
   a. Ohio has many farms
   b. Ohio has many rivers that are beautiful
   c. Ohio has fewer farms than it had in the past. ✓
   d. Ohio is the birthplace of most presidents

3. **Ohio is called the "Buckeye State" because:**
   a. of the Buckeye leaves on the trees ✓
   b. many buckeye peas grow there
   c. it was named after a man
   d. it is overrun with buckeyes

4. **Akron is important as a center for:**
   a. soap
   b. wheat, oats and corn
   c. rubber ✓
   d. being a president's home

5. **In this article, the word "shipped" means:**
   a. sent only by boat
   b. sent to other places ✓
   c. sent by mail
   d. ships are an important product

6. **Since Ohio has many big cities, we can guess:**
   a. there are no small towns
   b. all of the forests are gone
   c. there are no horses
   d. that many people live in cities ✓

Page 78

Baseball is often called the national **pastime** because it is so popular in the United States. During the spring and summer months millions of people play this exciting game, while millions of others watch the game and follow the progress of their favorite teams and players.

Baseball began in the eastern United States in the mid 1800's. The National League was founded in 1876 and the American League in 1900.

The game has now **spread** to other parts of the world. It is a major sport in such countries as Canada, Italy, Japan, Taiwan, The Netherlands, South Africa and many Latin American countries. There are organized baseball teams for every age group from 8-year olds to adults.

1. **The best title for this story is:**
   a. Baseball in America
   b. Baseball, An International Sport ✓
   c. The History of Baseball
   d. The Most Popular Sport in the World

2. **Baseball season is mostly:**
   a. the spring months
   b. the fall
   c. the summer months
   d. spring and summer months ✓

3. **Baseball is called a "pastime" because:**
   a. it began in the past
   b. it takes a lot of our most important time
   c. people spend a lot of time watching or playing it ✓
   d. it isn't as important as it was in the past

4. **The article says:**
   a. older people enjoy the sport most
   b. most people just watch
   c. anyone from 8 years of age may join a team ✓
   d. Americans are the best players

5. **The word "spread" as used above means:**
   a. moved to other places ✓
   b. plays baseball
   c. thinks the sport is exciting
   d. put on with a knife

6. **After reading the article we can say the author:**
   a. goes to many games
   b. plays baseball
   c. thinks the sport is exciting ✓
   d. wishes less time were devoted to baseball

Page 79

California is **probably** the fastest growing state in the Union. Millions of people live here now who did not live here ten years ago.

The Spaniards were the first to explore and settle California. They named Los Angel[es] and San Francisco.

In 1849, gold was discovered in California and many Americans came to seek riche[s]. Farmers came to raise crops in the warm climate. Men came to make movies becau[se] the sunny weather allowed them to take pictures outdoors nearly every day. Later, [oil] was discovered and people came to work in the oil fields.

California has many miles of coastline and is therefore a leader in commercial fishin[g].

1. **The best title for this story is:**
   a. A Beautiful State
   b. Land of the Free
   c. California, Today and Yesterday ✓
   d. The Largest State

2. **The first people who came to settle California were:**
   a. Spaniards ✓
   b. oil workers
   c. movie makers
   d. farmers

3. **The story mentions the farmers just after it tells about:**
   a. the oil workers
   b. the fisherman
   c. the discovery of gold ✓
   d. the movie makers

4. **The word "probably" means:**
   a. most likely ✓
   b. in many cases
   c. definitely
   d. surely

5. **Oilmen, farmers, movie makers and others probably like California most because of the:**
   a. view
   b. many cities
   c. parks and beaches
   d. climate ✓

Page 80

© Frank Schaffer Publications, Inc.

124

FS-32045 Readi[ng]

Answer Key

A spider is a small, eight-legged animal. Spiders spin webs of silk. They use the webs to catch insects for food.

All spiders spin silk, but some kinds do not make webs. A good example of this is the bolas spider who spins a single line of silk. At the end he spins a drop of sticky silk. He swings this line at a nearby insect and traps it in the ball.

All spiders have fangs and most have poison glands. A spider's bite can kill insects and many other small animals, but few spiders are harmful to man. Many people are afraid of spiders, but only hurt or frightened spiders bite man.

Spiders are helpful to man because they eat harmful insects such as locusts which destroy crops, and flies and mosquitos which carry diseases.

1. The main reason for writing this article was to tell about:
   a. spiders' webs
   b. helpful spiders
   c. poisonous spiders
   d. spiders in general

2. All spiders:
   a. make webs
   b. spin silk
   c. have fangs
   d. both B and C

3. Most spiders:
   a. are harmful
   b. have poison glands
   c. kill humans
   d. spin silk for clothing

4. A poisonous spider's bite is most harmful to:
   a. small animals and insects
   b. man
   c. frightened children
   d. dogs

5. In this story the word "drop" means:
   a. allow to fall
   b. a small bit of water
   c. a very small amount
   d. a steep cliff with land far below

6. When you aren't sure a spider is harmless it is best to:
   a. put it in a jar
   b. call the fire department
   c. leave it alone
   d. pick it up and take it to school to study

Name _____ Date _____

Read each paragraph. Decide which answer tells the main idea and circle it.

1. Somebody is moving in under my front porch today. Only it's not a somebody. It's a somebuggy. A whole lot of somebuggies, to be exact! I watched quietly from the top of the stairs. A family of 300 ants came marching along. First in line were the baby ants. They looked very tired.
   a. a moving porch   b. somebuggies moving day   c. the somebuggy march

2. The biggest ant led the way, I called him Chief. He directed all the traffic. It was a good thing Chief had six legs. He could point six different ways at once. Here. There. Left. Right. Straight ahead. In no time, Chief had all the baby ants moved into their rooms.
   a. how many legs ants have
   b. directing ant traffic
   c. what a Chief does

3. Next came the worker ants. They carried all the food. Tiny pieces of cupcake, bread, potato chips and one olive passed right by my nose. Well, well! I'll bet someone in the park is missing his picnic lunch. The last ant had a tiny box on his back. It was a Bingo game.
   a. picnic lunch   b. games worker ants play   c. what worker ants carry

4. Last in line was the Queen. Fifteen ants held an umbrella over her. Ants get hot, too, I guess. At last, the ants were all moved in. I hope they don't make a lot of noise. It's fun having somebuggy under my porch. Maybe some more somebuggies will move in tomorrow.
   a. my new neighbors
   b. why ants get hot
   c. coming of the Queen

—Thinking Time—

Read the next two questions carefully. Answer them on the back of this paper.

1. Ants often have to move to new homes or "nests". Why do they probably have to move?
2. Ants are insects. They have six legs. Name other insects that you know about or have caught.

Soccer claims to be the most popular sport in the world. Over one hundred and forty nations belong to its international federation. Other nations also play the game but do not enter international competition.

Every four years the best national soccer teams in the world gather for almost a month to compete for the World Cup.

In 1974, 16 teams competed for the Cup. Defending champion, Brazil, competed against host nation, Germany and 14 other countries. The United States failed to qualify for the World Cup. In the championship game the strong defensive team of West Germany met the strong offensive team from The Netherlands. The West German team was victorious.

1. The best title for this article is:
   a. The U.S. Joins Soccer
   b. American Soccer Teams
   c. Soccer, A Major Sport
   d. Learning to Play Soccer

2. The story says that:
   a. The U.S. is a major soccer power
   b. The U.S. is not interested
   c. The U.S. tried but did not qualify for the World Cup
   d. The U.S. will qualify someday

3. The winner of the World Cup in 1974 was:
   a. The United States
   b. The Netherlands
   c. West Germany
   d. Russia

4. The former champion was:
   a. West Germany
   b. Brazil
   c. The Netherlands
   d. East Germany

5. In the article above, the word "claims" means:
   a. pieces of ground to be farmed
   b. it is so
   c. it is said to be so
   d. an amount of money owed

6. It is possible to assume that:
   a. this sport is gaining people's interest
   b. soccer will continue to be popular
   c. other countries will join the competition in the future
   d. all of these are true

Name _____

On the surface a submarine operates much like any other ship. It has a rudder and stern and can be handled like other surface ships.

In order to dive, the submarine takes water into its ballast tanks by releasing air pressure that kept the water out.

When it is submerged, it switches to battery-driven electric motors. Nuclear-powered submarines continue to use their normal engines. By adjusting its diving planes, the sub can move up and down in the water. The submarine sets its diving planes to rise and blows all the water from its ballast tanks.

1. The best title for this article is:
   a. How Submarines Submerge
   b. How Submarines Operate
   c. How Subs Rise
   d. Parts of a Submarine

2. Submarines may be handled much like other ships when:
   a. they are submerged
   b. they are on the surface
   c. the ballast tanks are full

3. Submarines dive by:
   a. letting out the air pressure
   b. filling the tanks with fish
   c. emptying the ballast tanks
   d. putting up the periscope

4. The diving planes are used to help the sub:
   a. move up and down in the water
   b. to fly
   c. to help the sub rise
   d. both A and C

5. In this story, the word "switches" means:
   a. buttons to push
   b. changes
   c. things that can cause a machine to work
   d. connections to lights

6. Probably the parts of a submarine that make it most unlike other ships are the:
   a. rudders
   b. the ballast tanks
   c. the sterns
   d. the nuclear power

Butterflies are the most beautiful of the insects. Poets have called them "winged flowers" and "flying gems." They are found throughout the world.

It is hard to believe that a beautiful butterfly was once a wormlike caterpillar. Caterpillars hatch from the eggs of butterflies and later turn into butterflies. Although the caterpillar eats leaves and fruit and can harm crops, the butterfly does no harm because it can't bite or chew.

Butterflies do not grow in size as they get older. They remain the same size throughout their lifetimes.

No one knows why they are called butterflies. Perhaps it is because many of them are bright yellow like butter.

1. A good title for this story is:
   a. Harmful Caterpillars
   b. Catching Butterflies
   c. Beautiful Insects
   d. The Habits of Butterflies

2. The story says that butterflies remain the same:
   a. size
   b. form
   c. colors
   d. shape

3. The caterpillar is more harmful to crops than:
   a. the butterfly
   b. worms
   c. other insects
   d. small animals

4. Butterflies got their name because of:
   a. their color
   b. an unknown reason
   c. the fact that they looked like butter
   d. their softness

5. In this story, the word "bright" means:
   a. well lit
   b. a light or brilliant color
   c. smart
   d. colorful

6. Poets gave special names to butterflies because:
   a. they always make up names
   b. the names sounded better than butterfly
   c. they thought they were as pretty as flowers and jewels
   d. the new names were easier to write

Name _____

A seal is a sleek animal with a body shaped like a bullet. Seals are excellent swimmers and divers. They spend most of their time in the water, but give birth to their young on land.

Some seals migrate about 5,000 miles each year. During the entire trip, the seal swims from 10 to 100 miles from shore, never stopping to touch land. No one knows why they make this long yearly trip.

Men hunt seals for their fur and meat which can be used for animal food, poultry food and fertilizer. Seal blubber may be used for cooking or burned for light and heat.

1. The best title for this article is:
   a. The Value of Seals
   b. Seals
   c. Why Men Hunt Seals
   d. Where Seals Live

2. Most seals live in:
   a. zoos and circuses
   b. fresh water
   c. lakes and ponds
   d. oceans or inland seas

3. Seal babies are born:
   a. in the water
   b. in a special nest
   c. on land
   d. in the ocean

4. Men hunt seals because:
   a. they want their fur
   b. they want the meat
   c. their blubber is useful
   d. all of these reasons

5. The word "migrate" means:
   a. swim
   b. eat
   c. travel
   d. have babies

6. Although man doesn't really understand why seals migrate, the seal probably:
   a. does it because he likes to swim long distances
   b. likes the foods in other places
   c. likes a vacation
   d. has a reason known only to other seals

Answer Key

Page 89

Name ___ Date ___

Read each paragraph. Decide which answer best tells the main idea and circle it.

1. I started out as a seed, but a very special seed, as you will see. One day (before it was a bud) little leaves sprang out of the ground. Yup! It was Spring. Time for leaves to grow.
   - **(a) beginning of Spring**
   - b. a warm day
   - c. when the earth starts to grow

2. Pretty soon, it was my turn to make an appearance. At first, I was a little bud on a big leaf. All day, I just sat around in the sun. What a life! I got bigger, fatter and rounder. I looked terrific!
   - a. sitting in the sun all day
   - **(b) a big, fat leaf**
   - c. life as a leaf

3. Farmer Mike walked through the fields. He stopped right near my vine. "What happened here?" he asked, scratching his head. "A purple pumpkin in my patch! I'm afraid no one will want that one for Halloween."
   - a. Farmer Mike's patch
   - b. a Halloween pumpkin
   - **(c) a strange pumpkin**

4. Oh sob! Halloween night all alone. I'm a failure as a pumpkin. Later on, Missy Tissy came to the patch. She tripped over my stem and screamed: A GIANT GRAPE. The whole world will want to see this! I felt so happy. I really wasn't a pumpkin after all.
   - a. all alone on Halloween
   - **(b) a happy ending**
   - c. a screaming grape

—Thinking Time—
Read the next two questions carefully. Answer them on the back of the paper.
1. Pumpkins are big, round, orange and grow on a vine. Describe everything you can about a banana.
2. In Spring everything starts to bloom and grow. What begins to happen to plants, trees and flowers in the Fall?

Page 88

Name ___ Date ___

Read each paragraph. Decide which answer best tells the main idea and circle it.

1. Have you ever heard someone say: "He's wise as an owl?" Owls may look wise but they really aren't. Now take the elephant. He learns very quickly. You always see elephant acts at the circus. But have you ever seen owl acts?
   - a. a smart bird
   - **(b) a funny saying**
   - c. a circus act

2. With your fingerprints, you can make all different kinds of faces. Dot a few dots, draw some lines and your prints can say many things: happy, sad, angry, afraid, worried. A fingerprint can even become a ladybug or a turtle. Make some fingerprints of your own. Draw in pictures of other animals.
   - a. how many fingers you have
   - b. how to draw a face
   - **(c) things to make from fingerprints**

3. If you see a red spider, make a wish, quick! Then jump around in a circle on one foot. Make a sound just like a mad bee. Whirligigs have funny names. There are so many... count to 25 three times. Now, if you can still remember what you wished for, it will come true tomorrow.
   - **(a) the red spider wish**
   - b. how to make wishes
   - c. how to fly backwards

4. Why is a butterfly called a butterfly? He can fly, that's for sure. But he's not made of butter. Are there only "lady" ladybugs? Nope. There are as many male-ladybugs as lady-ladybugs. There must be better names for butterflies and ladybugs.
   - a. insects with funny names
   - b. insects made of butter
   - **(c) giving an insect a new name**

—Thinking Time—
Read the next two questions carefully. Answer them on the back of this paper.
1. If you wanted something very much, what would you do to make your wish come true?
2. A rabbicoon is part rabbit and part raccoon. From the names of the next four animals, make up two silly names and get two new animals: kangaroo, moose, turtle, seal.

Page 87

Name ___ Date ___

Read each paragraph. Decide which answer best tells the main idea and circle it.

1. Most animals have tails. But many other things have tails, too. Kites have tails made of string. An airplane's tail helps it to fly. The bottom of your shirt has a tail, but it doesn't help you fly. Lots of little girls wear pigtails—but they don't look anything like a pig's tail.
   - a. funny names for tails
   - **(b) different kinds of tails**
   - c. why we have tails

2. Did you know your eyebrows can talk? Lifted way up, they say "Surprise!" Down, way down, says you're mad. Move them together so they meet across your nose. That means you are worried. Next time you look in a mirror, make a face. Did your eyebrows say anything?
   - **(a) how eyebrows talk**
   - b. how to make eyebrows move
   - c. watching your eyebrows

3. Have you ever seen a whirligig? It's a strange insect that lives in ponds. It spins around in water like a mad bee. Whirligigs have funny eyes. Each eye has two halves. One half looks up. The other half looks down—at the same time. Don't try to catch a whirligig. They smell awful.
   - **(a) an unusual insect**
   - b. strange-looking eyes
   - c. how whirligigs smell

4. Black is many things. It's a night without stars. It's a shadow on the wall. It's the color of my eyes and the color of my hair. Black is my favorite color. Dot in all there is to that!
   - a. why shadows are black
   - **(b) many things that are black**
   - c. my favorite color of hair

—Thinking Time—
Read the next two questions carefully. Answer them on the back of this paper.
1. There are many different kinds of bags. How many different kinds of bags can you think of?
2. What is your favorite color? Think of three things of that color that are unusual.

Page 89

Name ___ Date ___

Read each paragraph. Decide which answer best tells the main idea and circle it.

1. Does anyone want a little sister? I've got one I'd like to give away. Yesterday, my Mom had to go shopping. "I'll be back at one o'clock. You take good care of Patty," she said. I asked Patty what she wanted to do. That was my first mistake.
   - a. giving sisters away
   - b. sitting on my sister
   - **(c) babysitting a little sister**

2. Patty wanted only a Queen Supreme hamburger. I said, "No that's too far away. It's Heavenly Hamburgers—or nothing!" Patty sat in the front of the bus. I sat in the back. Suddenly, she started to cry—real loud. "I've been on death!" The lady gave me a mean look. We went to Queen Supreme after all.
   - a. eating on the bus
   - **(b) Patty gets her way**
   - c. Patty's favorite hamburger

3. Queen Supreme was very crowded. We had to wait. A man gave Patty a Burger Boat to make. I told her not to sail it—or else! She did it anyway. It landed right in some baby's milkshake. The baby screamed. I crawled under the table.
   - **(a) getting into trouble**
   - b. making babies scream
   - c. the trouble with Burger Boats

4. Back home, Patty brought her Bing-Bang game into the living room—and tripped. How was I going to clean up 3,000 marbles? Just then Mom came home. "Look what he did!" Patty cried. I went to my room and locked the door. In three days, I might come out again, but not before.
   - a. making sisters happy
   - b. a long rest
   - **(c) a crazy day**

—Thinking Time—
Read the next two questions carefully. Answer them on the back of this paper.
1. Pretend you are baby-sitting for Patty. Name 3 things you would do to keep her out of trouble.
2. Patty said her brother ruined her game. What do you think their mother said?

Page 91

Name ___ Date ___

Read each paragraph. Decide which answer best tells the main idea and circle it.

1. An elephant is very lucky. He carries his shower around with him. If an elephant gets dirty, he can just turn on his trunk. There is one funny thing about elephants, though. First, they get themselves all clean. Then they go sit in the mud. I wish I could do that, too.
   - a. how elephants clean their trunks
   - b. when elephants take showers
   - **(c) some funny things about elephants**

2. Have you ever seen: An ox in a box? A clam eating ham? A duck saying "cluck"? A fly wearing a tie? A moose flying on a goose? A seal shopping for a meal? Or a bear with blonde curly hair?
   - **(a) some strange animals**
   - b. animals I've seen
   - c. new animals to see

3. Click! Your pen is ready to write. Long ago, getting ready to write was not so easy. Everyone had to make their own pens, called quills. Quill pens were made from feathers. Turkey feathers were used most often. But a swan feather made the best pen.
   - a. the best kind of pen
   - **(b) pens used long ago**
   - c. feathers made from pens

4. I'm making a cake for my sister's birthday. Am I nice! Now watch carefully. You might want to make my Oozie Doozie Cake someday. Start with 2 cups mint chip ice cream. Add 4 grapes, 1 cup smashed peas, 25 eggs, chopped lettuce and some peanut butter. That's it.
   - a. making green ice cream
   - b. an Oozie Doozie boy
   - **(c) making a birthday cake**

—Thinking Time—
Read the next two questions carefully. Answer them on the back of this paper.
1. Use the next five animal names and make them do something strange, like the animals in story #2: Cat, frog, cow, ant, bunny.
2. If you could make your favorite cake, what five things would it have in it?

Page 90

Name ___ Date ___

Read each paragraph. Decide which answer best tells the main idea and circle it.

1. Yesterday I passed by Connie's Candy Corner. They are having a contest. "Win a Whizzer Bike," the sign read. "Just guess the number of jelly beans in this jar. Bring in your guess and drop it in the box before 5 o'clock on Thursday."
   - **(a) a Win-A-Bike contest**
   - b. guessing jelly beans
   - c. winning a contest

2. How am I going to win that contest? Hm-m-m-m. I've got it! I'll buy a jar just like the one in the candy store. Then I'll buy some jelly beans. One by one I'll drop them into the jar until it is full. My little sister can write down the numbers. Her reward for helping me will be fifteen red jelly beans.
   - **(a) planning a contest**
   - b. a plan to win
   - c. a way to count

3. At last, the day arrived. Everyone crowded into the candy store at 4 o'clock. "We have a tie," Connie announced. "Fourteen people guessed the same number! I wonder how that happened? We'll just have to have a tie-breaker." Everyone who was correct, get ready!
   - a. how to break ties
   - b. fourteen guesses
   - **(c) winning tie**

4. Connie lifted out another jar. It was filled with peanuts. "Everyone gets one guess—right now!" My guess didn't win— was off by 600 peanuts. Oh, well. At least I have 1304 jelly beans to eat when I get home.
   - a. how I lost the contest
   - **b. the number of peanuts**
   - c. a winner by 600 peanuts

—Thinking Time—
Read the next two questions carefully. Answer them on the back of this paper.
1. I lost the contest, but that's OK. I'll enter another contest tomorrow. I like contests. What is the main idea of this story?
2. Read #4. Why did Connie have everyone guess the number of peanuts right then?

FS-32045 Reading

Answer Key

Page 93

Read each paragraph. Decide which answer best tells the main idea and circle it.

1. "Well here we are," said City Rat. "It's nice to be at the beach for a change." City Rat banged on a bell. "A room, please—for 80," he told Beach Rat. "Nice hotel you have here. How's the garbage? Good? Well, that's fine. We'll take a table in the alley at 8 o'clock. See you then."
   a. moving to the beach
   b. where rats live
   (c.) rats on a vacation

2. Do you want to be a Bee-For-A-Day? Go see Wacky Wendy. She'll turn you into one. Wendy has a Magic Insect Maker in her room. This is how she makes Bee Brew. Start with grape juice. Add 4 fingernails and 16 hairs. Put in a pinch of dust and some bubble bath. Shake hard.
   a. how insects are brewed (b.) magic Bee Brew c. a grape and dust elephant

3. One day, I saw a mouse near the P.Z.B & M Market. He looked so lonely. I invited him to come home with me. That night he went to sleep by my window. Next morning: "What is this?" my mother screamed. "Your mouse has invited his whole family over here! I guess I should be glad you didn't find a lonely elephant and bring him home!"
   (a.) a mouse that found an elephant
   b. a lonely mouse finds a home
   c. scaring my mother

4. "I'm sorry, Arthur. Doug can't come out and play," his father said. "Late last night, it finally happened. Doug turned into a TV. We called the doctor. He couldn't do a thing for Doug. I guess we'll have to wait until he blows a tube. Then maybe he'll turn back into Doug again."
   a. blowing a tube (b.) what happened to Doug c. getting sick from TV

Thinking Time
Read the next two questions carefully. Answer them on the back of this paper.
1. If you were only five inches tall, what would you be? What would you do or that you can't do now?
2. Why did Doug turn into a TV? Draw a picture of what he probably looked like.

Page 94

Read each paragraph. Decide which answer best tells the main idea and circle it.

1. I heard my dog Wolfgang barking. He was down in the basement. There's a ghost living down there, you know. I wondered if he caught my dog. Wolfgang barked louder and louder. He sounded frightened. I thought, "I must save him!"
   a. frightened dog
   b. a lost boy
   (c.) a barking ghost

2. Slowly, I opened the basement door. I had my mother's mop, just in case. Wolfgang stopped barking, but I couldn't see him anywhere. It was mostly dark, only a little sunlight. Something moved! It was near the washing machine. WHAM! I hit a pile of clothes. WHAM, again. "Where's my dog!" I yelled.
   (a.) hunting for a dog b. mopping up clothes c. hitting piles of clothes

3. Clothes were everywhere! I spilled some soap, too. But no ghost. Did I miss him? Next I crept over to an open window. I had my mop all ready to clobber the ghost. Suddenly, something licked my nose. It was Wolfgang! He had escaped from the ghost.
   a. the clothes escape
   b. escaping out of windows
   (c.) the return of Wolfgang

4. A minute later, my Mom turned on the light. She was not very happy. Her clean wash was all over the floor. I explained to her about the terrible ghost. "But I got him! I hit him with this mop. WHAM. He'll never come back here again. I saved Wolfgang's life. Aren't you proud of me?"
   a. how to scare a ghost (b.) a very brave boy c. a very mad mother

Thinking Time
Read the next two questions. Answer them on the back of this paper.
1. Clothes were everywhere! What other way can you spell the underlined word? Use it in a sentence.
2. When somebody is said to be "white as a ghost," how do you think that person looks and feels?

Page 95

Read each paragraph. Decide which answer best tells the main idea and circle it.

1. Here's a trick to try on one of your friends. Have her stand against a wall. The right side of her shoe and her shoulder are against the wall. Now ask her to lift her left leg off the floor. Could she do it?
   (a.) playing a trick on a friend
   b. the best place for doing tricks
   c. trying out tricks on a wall

2. "Why are you boys fighting?" their mother asked. "I told you two boys to share the sled." "Jack insisted that he was sharing. "Not really," his mother said. "You always get the sled going down. Tony only gets it coming up. That's not exactly what I would call a fair share."
   a. learning to share (b.) an unfair share c. a sled for two

3. Finish this rhyme:
   Three tall men were sitting in a tree.
   An owl came along and sat on one knee.
   "Don't stay here, this is not your nest,
   (a.) making up the end of a rhyme
   b. finding a word to rhyme with nest
   c. finishing a story about trees

4. "Thanksgiving Day comes inn November. My family meats for dinner at 4 o'clock. Last year, my Dad red a special story. I wish he wood do it again this year." Some words in the story are not spelled correctly. Can you find them? Cross them out. Write the correct spelling above the word.
   a. two ways to spell (b.) finding misspelled words c. a spell-binding story

Thinking Time
Read the next two questions carefully. Answer them on the back of this paper.

Page 96

Name ___   Date ___
Read each paragraph. Decide which answer best tells the main idea and circle it.

1. My dad has a rule: No one leaves the dinner table until everyone finishes eating. You might think that's a good rule. But you don't know my little brother. His name is Jeff. I think Jeff is half-snail. He is very slow.
   a. eating at a table
   (b.) a dinner time rule
   c. little boys who eat snails

2. Last night we had peas for dinner. Jeff ate all his peas—one-by-one! Then we had hot cheese sandwiches. Jeff took 50 teeny tiny bites, then held up the sandwich. He chewed a capital T into the toast. One hour and Jeff still hadn't finished eating!
   a. peas and cheese for dinner b. how to make a T (c.) a very long dinner hour

3. Jeff is driving me crazy! I have to find a way to make him eat faster. Tonight, my favorite show, Long Lost Larry, is on TV. I'm working on a speedy-eating plan right now.
   (a.) a plan for Jeff b. a favorite TV show c. a boy goes crazy

4. We're having hamburgers for dinner—Jeff's favorite! "Let's have a contest," I said. "We'll make an 'I'. I'll make the line and you make the 'll.' Whoever finishes first gets to eat the whole 'I'. You should have seen Jeff eat! I let him win, of course. But tomorrow is going to be a problem. What kind of contest can you have eating turkey?"
   a. drawing "I's" on hamburgers
   b. eating hamburgers slowly
   (c.) an eat-fast contest

Thinking Time
Read the next two questions carefully. Answer them on the back of this paper.
1. Make up a long sentence using all four of these words: goat, trumpet, gum, skating.
2. "Jeff eats slowly. He swallows much too fast. It takes him hours to eat." One sentence doesn't fit. Cross it out and write another one that fits this story better.

Page 97

Name ___   Date ___
Read each paragraph. Decide which answer best tells the main idea and circle it.

1. Have you ever had a piece of shoo-fly pie? No, it is not made of flies. This pie got its name long, long ago. After baking, a pie was set by a window to cool. Flies could smell the pie miles away. Hundreds would zoom over. Somebody had to stand by the window and shoo the flies away all day.
   (a.) how shoo-fly pie got its name
   b. a good name for pies with flies
   c. why flies like shoo-fly pie

2. "Boy, I slept like a baby last night." That means that you probably slept for ten hours. Now you feel all rested. But, if you want to feel really, really rested—sleep like a gorilla! Gorillas sleep for fourteen hours at a stretch. They never even have time to get tired.
   a. how long babies sleep b. how to sleep soundly (c.) how to feel rested

3. Many people are afraid of sharks. They have good reason to be! A shark's tooth is as hard as steel. All other fish in the ocean steer clear of sharks. Why? A shark is always hungry. It could eat a whale and be hungry again an hour later. Sharks are sometimes called Deadly Demons. Now you know why.
   a. why sharks eat so much
   (b.) a fierce, frightening fish
   c. the deadliest animal of them all

4. The next time you sneeze, try not to close your eyes. No one has been able to do it yet. You may be the first. Do you know how fast that sneeze travels? About 100 miles per hour! You never knew your nose had so much power, did you?
   a. where a sneeze travels (b.) facts about sneezes c. facts about noses

Thinking Time
Read the next two questions carefully. Answer them on the back of this paper.
1. There is a cookie called a "snickerdoodle." Make up a story about how the cookie got its name.
2. "Sleep like a baby" means you sleep a long time. What does "sleep like a log" mean?

Page 98

Name ___   Date ___
Read each paragraph. Decide which answer best tells the main idea and circle it.

1. I'm going to tell you three things. Then you tell me who might say them: "How do you feel? Stick out your tongue. Say Ah-h-h." If you guessed a doctor, you're right. Word clues can help you name many different people. You know who they are by the special words they use. What would be some good clues for a teacher?
   a. finding the right words
   b. how to name a doctor
   (c.) a word clue game

2. There are many ways to discover new things. Experiments are a fun way to discover. Some experiments you can do easily at home. Others your teacher can help you do. Discovering things for yourself is exciting! All you have to do is watch, listen and try.
   a. experimenting at home (b.) ways to discover c. ways to do experiments

3. Two hundred years ago, your mother might have said: Go rub your teeth! Teeth were cleaned with chalk and a rag. Have you ever tasted chalk? Yeek! No wonder no one liked to clean their teeth. Chalk didn't do much good, either. It made teeth white, but it didn't get them clean.
   (a.) cleaning teeth long ago
   b. how chalk tastes
   c. how to clean your teeth

4. There was an old woman who lived in a tent. She had three dollars and 40 cents. "I need some carrots for my Foo-Fum stew. This money should buy me four thousand and two."
   a. how much carrots cost (b.) an old woman's wish c. when an old woman lives

Thinking Time
Read the next two questions. Answer them on the back of this paper.
1. Why would a toothbrush be much better than a rag for cleaning your teeth?
2. "A dinosaur once stood on my toe." Write the next line. The last word should rhyme with "toe."

Answer Key

Page 101

Name _____ **Date** _____

Read each paragraph. Decide which answer best tells the main idea and circle it.

1. While searching for my lost bike, my head brushed against a foot. It belonged to the giant, Jasper. He was fast asleep high in a tree. Jasper sleeps all summer long. Hot weather makes him very grouchy!
   a. sleeping through the summer
   (b.) a sleeping giant
   c. long summer days

2. Carefully, I climbed up the tree. One of Jasper's coat pockets clanged and banged in the wind. When the wind stopped, I jumped into his pocket. You won't believe what's in here! Has Jasper moved all his furniture out of his cave?
   a. climbing into a giant's pocket
   b. pockets full of wind
   (c.) a surprise in a pocket

3. Deep inside the pocket, Jasper's grandfather clock is still ticking. A bathtub, over to the left a little, has a set of encyclopedias stacked inside. Jasper's refrigerator and TV are here, too. What is this behind the sofa? Well! What do you know!
   a. furniture made for pockets
   b. hiding behind sofas
   (c.) a giant's furniture

4. My bike! I found it! But how am I going to get it out of this pocket? Here's my knife. That's it! I'll cut a big hole in Jasper's pocket. Everything is crashing to the ground, including me. I jumped on my bike and made a quick get-away. A few minutes later, Jasper fell out of the tree. All his furniture was crashed. Phew! I got away just in the nick of time.
   a. pockets with holes in them
   (b.) getting back a bike
   c. a giant gets away

— Thinking Time —

Read the next two questions carefully. Answer them on the back of this paper.

1. Hot weather makes Jasper grouchy and mean. Name three things that make you feel grouchy?
2. A hole is an opening. What is another way to spell the word "hole"? Write the meaning.

Page 101 (right)

Name _____ **Date** _____

Read each paragraph. Decide which answer best tells the main idea and circle.

1. Long, long ago, there was a family named O'Leary. They lived in a castle. One summer, the O'Learys wanted to go on vacation. "Our castle doesn't have any locks," Mr. O'Leary said. "We need to get a good dragon to guard our gold."
   a. planning a summer vacation
   (b.) looking for a castle guard
   c. where the O'Leary family lived

2. "Oliver is our finest dragon," said the pet forest owner. Mr. O'Leary didn't think Ollie looked very fierce. But he had big beady eyes—a sign of a good dragon. Ollie jumped out of his nest. He wagged his tail and picked up a toy bone. It rattled.
   (a.) picking out a dragon
   b. a friendly pet
   c. leaving the nest

3. "Good-bye, Ollie," waved the O'Learys. "Take good care of our castle and our gold." Early Sunday, three men sneaked up on the bridge. Ollie sat up on his tail. He tried to roar. It sounded like "yip-yip." He tried to breathe fire. Only a little steam poured out. Ollie cried.
   a. a very soft roar
   b. leaving for vacation
   (c.) trying to guard a castle

4. "Look, it's only a baby dragon!" The men felt sorry for Ollie. "Let's make him a hero." Inside the castle, the men tossed around some furniture. "Stand here in front of the gold, Ollie. The O'Learys will be home soon. They will think you scared us away." Ollie was so happy. Tomorrow he would practice his roar and his fire.
   (a.) a happy ending
   b. ruining a castle
   c. a little dragon comes home

— Thinking Time —

Read the next two questions. Answer them on the back of this paper.

1. In story #1, find a word that means "to take a trip." Now write two things about the last trip you took (even if it was just to the store).
2. How could you tell Ollie was just a baby dragon?

Page 99

Name _____ **Date** _____

Read each paragraph. Decide which answer best tells the main idea and circle it.

1. How would you like to have a flea circus? First of all, catch a bunch of fleas. Then make a little stage for the flea act. Fleas really can do tricks. They'll jump through hoops. They'll even pull a tiny paper wagon around!
   a. how fleas jump through hoops
   b. going to a flea circus
   (c.) putting on a flea circus

2. Do you see flashing lights over there? Those are fireflies. They really light up a dark sky. Try to catch some in a jar. Their light is so bright you could read this page by them.
   (a.) firefly facts
   b. reading by firefly light
   c. catching fireflies

3. There are hundreds of different kinds of ice cream. Rooty-Tooty is my favorite. This ice cream tastes good with everything; bananas, peas, hamburgers, toast and tomatoes, too. Tonight I'm having Rooty-Tooty Turkey. I warm up some Rooty-Tooty in a pan and pour it over the turkey. Best gravy in the whole world!
   a. ice cream that tastes like gravy
   b. how Rooty-Tooty Turkey tastes
   (c.) go-with-everything ice cream

4. The football game is over. Your friends are leaving the field. You want to know if your team won. There are two ways you could find out: Ask someone. Or, better, look at everyone's face. Do they look sad and unhappy? Now you can probably guess who won. Faces can tell all different feelings and moods without anyone saying a word.
   a. a winning team
   b. finding out who won
   (c.) what faces can tell you

— Thinking Time —

Read the next two questions. Answer them on the back of the page.

1. You are going to make an ice cream sundae. It is called Heaven-Help-Us. Name all the things you are going to put on your sundae.
2. John's bike was ruined. His brother left it out in the rain. Write a sentence or draw a picture to describe John's face.

Page 100

Name _____ **Date** _____

Read each paragraph. Decide which answer best tells the main idea and circle it.

1. There are many different things you can do with gum. Some of them are bad. Let's think of a few fun things first. You can chew it. You can blow bubbles. You could even fix a broken model airplane with some chewed gum (just in case you run out of glue).
   a. how gum is different
   (b.) the many uses of gum
   c. why gum is good

2. Now let's talk about the bad things. My friend Andy probably knows 132 different uses for gum—and not one is very good! Someday, I wouldn't be surprised if they pass Gum Laws because of Andy. He might even end up in jail for breaking gum laws!
   a. passing a Gum Law
   b. 132 uses for gum
   (c.) about Andy and gum

3. On wash day, Andy's mother found a pack of gum in his shirt pocket. But only after she pulled it out of the dryer! All the clothes were ruined! At night, Andy sticks his old gum under his bed. One day, the cat went to sleep under there. They had to call a vet to come over and cut off all the cat's fur. The cat had to wear a sweater after that.
   a. bad uses for gum
   b. where cats take a nap
   (c.) ruining clothes in the dryer

4. "That's it! The gum goes or you go!" Andy's mother stated. But Andy had an idea. He would make a Used Gum Holder. Every day he puts a piece of tape over his belt. This is how it works: Pull up piece of tape. Stick gum to belt. Smooth tape over again. At the end of day, tape will pull gum off belt. And that's the end of Andy's story.
   (a.) a good idea for gum
   b. taping gum to belts
   c. a very angry mother

— Thinking Time —

Read the next two questions carefully. Answer them on the back of this paper.

1. Andy would like to stop chewing gum. What could you invent for him to help him stop chewing? Draw a picture of it.
2. If some Gum Laws were really passed, name four DON'Ts that would be on the list for sure.

Page 102

Name _____ **Date** _____

Read each paragraph. Decide which answer best tells the main idea and circle it.

1. Norway is sometimes called the Land of the Midnight Sun. The sun shining at midnight? That's right. During June and July, the sun never sets. It is daytime all the time. But this happens for only two months. Just think how much electricity is saved.
   a. who lives in the Land of the Midnight Sun
   b. a place where it is daytime year round
   (c.) a place where the sun shines at midnight

2. Do you have a pesty little sister? I do. She used to come in my room a lot. But I fixed that! Do you want to know how to do it, too? Keep all kinds of squishy things in your room. Snails, worms, dead plants and a few snakes. My little sister doesn't even come near me any more!(Neither does anyone else!)
   (a.) keeping sisters out
   b. fixing your room
   c. sisters that are pests

3. Yesterday, I whacked my funny bone on a door. It wasn't the least bit funny! I could feel the pain all the way to my toes. This bone needs another name.
   a. a bone that is not fun
   b. a funny name for a bone
   (c.) a bone that hurts the toes

4. I had to write a story. The title was: Who Would You Like to Invite to Dinner? And this is what I wrote: I would like to ask a brontosaurus to dinner—every night. He loves vegetables and I don't. Our apartment is on the fifth floor. A brontosaurus is five stories tall, too. His mouth would fit perfectly at the kitchen window. That's why I would like to invite to dinner.
   a. a story about dinner
   (b.) the best guest
   c. dinner on the fifth floor

— Thinking Time —

Read the next two questions carefully. Answer them on the back of this paper.

1. Why would it be difficult to live where the sun shines all day and all night?
2. Hurt means _____. The opposite of this word is _____. How has someone hurt your feelings?

Page 103

Name _____ **Date** _____

Read each paragraph. Decide which answer best tells the main idea and circle it.

1. Guess what I am? I turn around, but I don't go anywhere. I'm fastened to a door and locked with a key. Sometimes I'm polished, sometimes I'm painted. Muddy hands and fingerprints are all over me.
   a. how to describe a lock
   (b.) a doorknob is described
   c. how to figure out riddles

2. "Kevin stop and dig a hole? Did he bury his feet? No. This is just a way to say. Some sayings are very funny. They help to describe what we are trying to say. Some sayings are very funny.
   (a.) why we use sayings
   b. sayings about plants
   c. how to plant feet

3. Poems about yourself are the best poems of all. Read this one. Then write another poem using your own name.
   S cott, Kentucky
   B orn in
   E nd of May is my birthday
   N ine years old
   a. short names
   (b.) poems about yourself
   c. words that rhyme with me

4. Joanie sent a message to her friends. They all belong to the Scutter Secret Club. This is what the note said: I don't feel 2 good. It must be something I 8. What was it—the black-14 P's or Mom's 5-layer cake? I'll go C a doctor. He'll know what 2 do 4 me.
   a. how Joanie got sick
   b. a person who can't spell
   (c.) writing a secret code

— Thinking Time —

Read the next two questions. Answer them on the back of this paper.

1. Make up some clues to describe a flag. Read them to a friend one-by-one. How many clues did you have to give before he guessed it?
2. Write your name or nickname down the side of a page just like #3. Now write a short poem telling something about yourself.

© Frank Schaffer Publications, Inc.

128

FS-32045 Readin